Louise C. Wicks
1st Edition 12-1995

GOOD MANNERS
for ~~Kids~~
young people

Louise Claude Wicks

WESTERN PRINTERS
Eugene, Oregon

Available From:

GOOD MANNERS FOR ~~KIDS~~ YOUNG PEOPLE

P.O. Box 11198

Eugene, OR 97440

ISBN No. 0-9649 470-0-5
Library of Congress Catalog Card Number: 95-90982

Production & Printing
Western Printers, Inc.
Eugene, Oregon

Illustrator
James Carpenter

Editor
Elizabeth Lyon

Acknowledgments

This book, like every nonfiction book, was dependent upon countless others helping me. Over and over I was asked, "What is a good manners reference book for my child?" and "Why don't you write one?" I cannot be articulate enough to express my heartfelt thank you to my many friends, clients, teachers, editor, publisher, librarians, business acquaintances, and those who have endorsed my book. A special thank-you goes to you young people who have been so enthusiastic with giving me suggestions, input and help.

Thank you especially to my daughter, grandchildren and my husband without whose support and encouragement I would never have been able to finish this book.

A special thank-you to Margaret Nichols, Superintendent of District 4J Schools; Ruth South, Librarian, University of Oregon; Linda M. Cheney, Owner/President of Cheney Financial Associates; Rabbi Efraim Davidson, Jewish Cultural Center; Father Theodore Berktold, St. Mary's Episcopal Church; Father Lee Owen, Anglican Church; Terry Hippenhammer, Director, Computing and Information Services, Eugene Public Schools; and the staff of the Episcopal Diocese of Oregon—Portland.

Contents

Introduction

Q: What do children and baby goats have in common?
A: They are both referred to as kids. They both need play, guidance, and love to become complete adults.

Q: How many times can you make a good first impression?
A: You have one time of less than three minutes to make a good first impression.

Q: If you are at the table eating and you need to blow your nose but you don't have a handkerchief or a tissue, is it okay to use your cloth napkin or paper napkin to blow your nose?
A: Neither one.

Q: If your meat is difficult to cut, do you hold your fork in your left hand by making a fist with which to hold it?
A: No. You never hold a utensil in a fist.

As a child or young adult, you may feel as if you live in a world of your own. This is not true. We all live in this world together.

Good manners help to smooth your way all through life.

Good manners are the accepted guidelines and rules of knowing the polite and courteous way of behaving in different everyday situations.

Good manners are a pleasant and enjoyable habit to be used every day, not only on special occasions.

Good manners are like your clothing. Without them you feel exposed and insecure.

If you practice good manners at home, they will become a pleasurable habit.

Ralph Waldo Emerson said,
"A great part of courage
is the courage of having done the thing before."

What Are Good Manners?

Good manners are the polite, thoughtful and acceptable way of behaving to help you get along with others. Bad manners means being unkind, inconsiderate or rude whether you mean to be or not. The most important key to good manners is to remember the golden rule: Treat others the way you would like to be treated. Always treat *all* other people the way you would like them to treat you. It is that simple. Being thoughtful and considerate of others is what manners are all about.

Basic good manners rules are the same no matter what your age. Learn and practice good manners now, and they will stand by you the rest of your life. Using good manners includes being:

Considerate—This means being respectful and thoughtful of all other peoples' feelings, no matter how different they are from you, what the color of their skin, what language they speak, what age they are, how much money you think they may have, or which religion they practice.

Courteous—This means being polite and using good manners. It means being thoughtful of others and showing kindness.

How do you learn to develop good manners? You start by studying this book with its many guidelines and rules of good manners. You can read them and refer to them as often as you need to remind yourself of the most polite and acceptable ways to behave. Then you practice, practice, practice. The more you practice your good manners, at home and out and about, the easier they become. As you practice, you will make good manners your good habits.

When good manners are a part of us, we don't have to consciously remember to "turn-on-good-manners" or use our "party-manners." When good manners are a part of us, we use them naturally under any conditions.

George Washington, our country's first president, was concerned with the way people treated other people. He wrote a book titled *Rules of Civility and Decent Behavior* giving 106 rules of etiquette for his time. These rules are still very good rules to follow today. Here are a few of them:

- *Not to pick one's teeth in public.*
- *Never spit, comb your hair, or fiddle with your fingernails in public.*
- *Always knock and receive permission before entering someone's home or someone's room.*
- *Always ask to borrow something from someone. Return the borrowed possession on time and in good repair.*
- *Close doors gently–don't slam them.*
- *Don't be an "elephant" going up and down stairs.*
- *Always arrive on time for a party or an appointment.*
- *Don't overstay your welcome.*
- *Always write thank-you notes.*

These rules are still as important and timely today as they were in George Washington's time.

Terms to Know

Etiquette: The conventional rules for conduct or behavior in a polite society. This is another word for "good manners."

Manners: A way of doing; a way of acting or behaving in the accepted customary way.

Mannerly: Having or showing good manners; being courteous and well-behaved.

Protocol: The acceptable way people representing a government should act. The written rules of etiquette for the diplomatic corps, military, royalty and heads of state for any country.

Basic Rules to Live By

- By treating others with respect and dignity you create a win-win situation.
- Think about fairness and honesty in everything that you do. Remember that no one likes cheaters of any kind so don't cheat at games or anything else. Even a "budge" (cut-in) in a line is cheating.
- Be trustworthy. Trust is a special unspoken bond between people. A trustworthy person does what they say they will do.
- Be considerate of others. Practice your manners and use them all the time so that you are never rude around others.
- Never make "fun" of others. Never point out, stare, make fun of, or make loud comments about a person with special needs or a person who is unusual in any way. Mentally put yourself in their situation. Treat them like you would like to be treated if you were in their same position. If a person has a physical restriction, for example, a wheel chair, and you think he or she would like help with a door, a curb or an elevator button, but you are not sure, ask if you can help. If they say "yes," help the best that you can. If they say "no," at least you offered.

Magic Words

Using these magic words form good habits and are pleasant to the ears:

"Please."

"Thank you."

"You are welcome."

"Excuse me."

"I'm sorry." (Be sure to use this only if you are sincere.)

Personal Habits

- Be a good listener. Don't interrupt when another person is talking, particularly with adults. Many times it's hard not to interrupt, but to do so is rude, thoughtless, and irritating to others. If you do have to interrupt another person, say, "Excuse me, but—" (then say whatever it is that is so important).

- Pick up after yourself and take care of your own mess.

- Take care of your own garbage and always use trash cans or appropriate receptacles. Recycle whenever possible.

- Cover your nose and mouth with a tissue, handkerchief, or your hand when you cough, sneeze, or yawn; then say, "Excuse me."

- If you burp or expel gas ("fart"), don't make a big deal about it. Just say, "Excuse me."

- Don't be "boisterous." This means don't be loud and always trying to draw attention to yourself when you're around others.

- Avoid nervous mannerisms such as drumming your fingers on the table, pulling your fingers at the joints or biting your fingernails. Don't pull or play with your hair, or comb your hair in public.
- Don't pick your nose or teeth in public.
- *Never spit.* Although some people do this to try to be "cool," spitting is really rude and disgusting. Not only does it spread germs, but it is gross to look at.

Compliments

When someone says something nice to you....

- Sincere compliments are pleasing to receive, and when you give a compliment you are showing a sensitive, thoughtful side of yourself.
- If you get a compliment, all you need to say is "Thank you." No need to "explain" anything.
- If you compliment someone on something they have or that they are wearing, *never* ask the person, "Where did you buy it?" or "How much did it cost?" If someone forgets and asks you the same questions, you don't need to feel obligated to answer. Just smile and change the subject or say, "I don't remember."
- Be sincere with your compliments. Remember the old adage, "If you can't say something nice then say nothing at all." Never give a compliment you don't really mean.

Different Language

- If you and a friend are speaking in a language that another friend does not understand, it's only courteous to explain to the friend who doesn't know the language what you have said. For example: If Maria and you are speaking Spanish in front of Tyler, who doesn't speak Spanish, explain what is being said. In this case you are the interpreter.

• You should interpret the conversation to the best of your ability. To interpret incorrectly could cause hurt and misunderstood feelings as well as a bad situation.

• Whether one or a group is speaking a different language, the conversation should be explained to others. Not to explain makes those speaking the different language seem secretive and rude.

Telling Secrets

Telling secrets to one friend when others are present is rude. It makes the one who tells the secret seem insecure and thoughtless. Also, it doesn't help the image of the one who continues to listen to the secrets. When it comes to telling secrets in front of others, don't be a part of it—either way. Think about how you feel when you are left out. Just don't allow yourself to be a part of hurting other's feelings.

Foul Language

You may on occasion be tempted to use foul language (dirty words). The best advice is: *don't*. Some kids think using foul language makes them "cool," but foul language really indicates a lack of vocabulary and a lack of "smarts." Others will have more respect for you and you'll have more respect for yourself if you simply keep your vocabulary "clean."

Hats

The rules of good etiquette say that if you're a boy or man you should *always* remove your hat or cap when you are inside. Even though you often see on TV or in the movies that men and boys keep their hats on, in "real life" this is not appropriate or socially acceptable. Wearing your hat or cap inside is rude.

When you are a boy and go to a restaurant or theater, you should check your hat in a coat-check room. If there is no coat-check room, place your hat under your chair or in the seat with you. Polite men and boys will always remove their hats when they are talking with an older person, particularly older women. Why "hats off" for men and boys and not for women and girls? It is an historic and cultural custom that had its beginnings in religious customs, and, though it may not seem "fair," it is socially acceptable for girls and women to keep their hats on when indoors. The exception is in places such as the theater where the hat blocks the view of those behind. When asked, the polite woman or girl will also remove her hat.

Personal Property

- Be respectful of other people's property.
- Never put your feet on furniture. (Footstools are the exception.)
- Never jump on furniture.
- Never sit on the arm of a chair or sofa.
- Never sit in a chair with the chair tipped back on the two back legs. Not only is that act unmannerly, but you could easily break a leg of the chair.
- Treat books with respect. Never mark or color in them, unless they are coloring books. Don't bend down pages, or leave them open when you are not using them. If you borrow a book, return it promptly.
- Don't be a "graffiti writer." Writing graffiti without permission is vandalism, which is breaking the law.
- Always knock and get permission before entering someone else's room or space.

Meeting and Greeting Others (Introductions)

When Should You Stand?

- Always stand for an introduction.
- Men, boys and young girls stand up when a woman comes into the room. You stand to show respect. You remain standing until the older woman is seated. When you are younger, it is sometimes hard to judge a person's age. A way to judge is: If the woman is about the same age as your mother or older, then stand. After all of the women are seated, then girls may sit down, and last of all men and boys.

Handshaking

- Always shake hands when being introduced.

- Handshaking is a universal sign of friendship. To intentionally refuse a handshake is known as an insult worldwide. When two people "give their word in good faith and shake hands," it means they will keep their word.

- In the past, women and girls were not expected to shake hands, but today women and girls shake hands with other women and girls as well as with men and boys.

- Practice handshaking so you are comfortable giving your hand when introduced.

- If you offer your hand and the other person doesn't offer theirs, then just put your hand down and don't make a big deal about it. The other person may not know good manners, or they may have a physical reason for not shaking hands. Whatever the reason, at least you offered your hand.

- A handshake should be firm, but not bone crushing or semi-wrestling. A handshake should be just like a count of 1, 2, 3. Don't make it a pumping exercise. The motion should be from the elbow. The "V" between the thumbs and forefingers should come together.

The "V" area between your thumb and forefinger is called a web. Your web and the other person's web should touch.

- Never shake hands with royalty. It is rude to try to do so, unless they offer their hand first.

Being Introduced

- Learn to greet people nicely, and when others speak to you answer them with words.

- Man, woman, boy or girl, no matter what your age is, *you should always stand for an introduction* and always look at the person to whom you are being introduced.

- If you don't understand the name of the person being introduced, you should ask that person to repeat his or her name. If you don't quite understand, you may ask again.

• You should speak clearly (no mumbling) when you are being introduced and when you are doing the introducing. Be friendly and confident.

• When you are introduced, use this absolutely correct, formal response no matter what your age: "How-do-you-do." However, to say "Hello" is perfectly acceptable and is what many people say. When you are introduced to other children, it's okay to just say "Hi." Even though "Hi" is not proper to use with adults, it is becoming more acceptable among children. But try to remember to say "Hello" or "How-do-you-do," particularly to older adults.

Introducing Yourself

• If your friends don't remember to introduce you, you should introduce yourself. Also, sometimes adults forget to use good manners and don't introduce children to adults or children to children. If this happens, introduce yourself, by saying "Hello," giving your name and immediately putting your hand out to shake hands. Example: "Hello! I'm Sam Garibaldi."

• When you introduce yourself and the other person doesn't give you his name, it's proper to say, "And what is your name?" If others introduce themselves to you, always give them your name. If you don't quite understand a name exactly, it is proper to ask the person to please repeat his or her name again.

• When you are introduced to someone, it's nice if you can think of something to say to each other rather than just stand and stare at each other. (Adults also often have this problem.) Maybe ask the other person where he is from, what grade he is in, if he likes to skate, where he lives, whatever comes to mind. Think about what you would like to be asked and ask those questions.

Introducing Friends to Other Friends

- You should *always introduce your friends to each other* right away, so they don't feel left out or unwanted.

- When introducing friends to other friends, the girl's name is said first because you are *presenting the boy to the girl*. A boy or man is presented to a woman or girl. That is the proper etiquette, no matter what age. Example: "Kate Hamilton, this is Chad Rodman."

- If you can't remember whose name comes first—just introduce them—don't worry about whose name comes first. Practice—then next time you'll remember. What is important is that you've introduced your friends to each other.

- If you can't remember last names, don't be embarrassed. This happens to adults also. Just say, "Kate, this is Chad." An introduction using only first names is better than no introduction. Confess that you can't remember their last names; then they will tell you their last names once again.

Introducing Younger People to Older People

- You always introduce a younger person to an adult, including adults in your family. Examples: "Mother, this is Shannon Williams." "Shannon, this is my mother, Mrs. Swenson." This also lets your friend know what name they are to call your parent. "Grandmother Lou, this is my friend, Bryan McDowell." "Bryan, this is my grandmother, Mrs. Boyer." Bryan should call your grandmother Mrs. Boyer unless your grandmother gives him permission to call her by the name you use for her. Example: "Mrs. Lee, this is Jessica Jones." "Jessica, this is Mrs. Lee, my friend Shawn's grandmother." When you add the extra information, your friends are able to make a connection in their minds. If there is no ready connection or you can't think of one quickly, don't worry about it.

- Always call an adult by Mr., Mrs., or Ms., or Miss. If adults give you permission to call them by their first names, then, of course, do so. Sometimes an aunt, uncle or grandparent may give your friends permission to use the name you call them. Example: "Rachel and Ellen, Kate calls me Aunt Beverly. You may also call me Aunt Beverly, if you wish."

Group Introductions

- Small Group: When you introduce a person to a small group, you say everyone's name as you introduce them and they shake hands. A small group has up to four or five people.

- Large Group: When you introduce a person to a large group, you might say, "Everyone, this is Lee Sung." Then you ask everyone to please introduce themselves. Everyone should, in turn, step up, introduce themselves and shake hands. Example: "Hello, Lee, I'm Adam Williams" (shaking hands). Next shaking hands, "Hello, I'm Jonathan Jacobs and please tell me again your name."

- Large Group with an Adult in Charge: If the large group has an adult in charge, then you would introduce your friend to the adult in charge first. Example: "Mr. Mendoza, this is Lee Sung; Lee, this is Mr. Alejandro Mendoza. He is our leader."

Acknowledging Arrivals of Others' Friends

Perhaps you are watching TV or playing with a friend. If an adult or another friend of your friend comes into the room, you should turn away from the TV or stop playing with your friend. Stand up, greet the friend, put your hand out to shake hands and say "Hello, Mrs. Velasquez." If you do not know who the person is, just say "Hello" and shake hands and give her your name. He or she should automatically tell you a name. Once that formality and greeting is taken care of, you may return to whatever you were doing. You have acknowledged the person's presence in your home or your friend's home. Both boys and girls should greet their parents' friends this way. If you have a brother or sister, younger or older, it is not necessary to go through the part of handshaking to greet their friends. However, it is required that you look up from what you are doing and say "Hello, Cole and Nonda" as a way of acknowledging that someone other than family has entered the room.

Meeting Important People

- If you are not sure what to do, using the term Mr., Miss, or Mrs. is always proper.

- Always shake hands, unless you are meeting royalty. Then, a bow or curtsey is appropriate. (See the next section.)

- An ambassador, governor, mayor, senator or lower-court judge are addressed using their title: Examples: "How do you do, Governor Jenkins." "How do you do, Judge Jacoby." "How do you do, Ambassador Smith."

- A judge of the Supreme Court is addressed as "Justice." Example: "How do you do, Justice O'Connor."

- An important person's wife or husband does not use

Never offer to shake hands with royalty. It is rude for you to try to do so unless they offer their hand first.

the title of the important person to whom they are married. Example: Governor Granetelli's wife is addressed as Mrs. Granetelli; Governor Granetelli's husband is addressed as Mr. Granetelli.

• If you are to meet the President or Vice-President of the United States there will be someone official to tell you what to do, when to do it, and what to say.

• If you meet an important person in your home, or at a friend's house, don't sit down until after the important person is seated.

• If you are at a party or reception for an important person, be sure that you meet the guest of honor first before you go talk to someone else.

• If you don't know anyone, you should introduce yourself to other guests, and shake hands. Adults will be pleased with you and younger people will be glad to have someone with whom they can talk.

• Don't think of grown-up parties as boring. You often meet very interesting people at some of these affairs. Use them as a place and time to practice your manners. Make an effort to be sociable. It is the guests' duty to circulate and be friendly and interested in other people.

• It is up to you to be outgoing and interesting for others to meet but never a "show off" or the center of attention.

• If you are meeting clergy (someone official from a church or synagogue), you may use their name and title in your greeting. If you know a title but not a name, just use the title. Examples: "How do you do, Rabbi Sherman," "How do you do, Rabbi," "How do you do, Father" (for bishop or priest), "How do you do, Father Smith," "How do you do, Bishop Jones," "How do you do, Pastor Johnson." A rabbi's wife or protestant minister's wife is simply called "Mrs." with her last name. The title "The Reverend" is used only on an envelope.

- Some churches have women clergy. Sometimes they are referred to by the same titles as the men clergy. Sometimes they have different titles. The acceptable, and the best, way to find out what they like to be called is to ask them.

Bow or Curtsy

- A "bow" is done by a boy and a "curtsy" is done by a girl. It is done as a show of respect to an adult of some great importance or to someone much older, such as your grandparents' age, or to royalty.

- How to bow: Bend from the waist. Allow your arms to remain straight but not stiff and to slide down the sides of your body. Bend approximately one-third of the distance between your straight position and 90° to your waist position. A bow lasting about the count of three is long enough.

- How to curtsy: Place the toes of your right foot behind your left heel, and a little to the left of the heel. Then bend your knees. Dip down, not too far, to about the count of two, then come up. (If you feel a little unsteady, press your right knee against the back of your left knee.) As you start your curtsy, extend your right hand to the distinguished person to whom you are curtsying. They shake your hand as you dip. If it is an occasion of not shaking hands (such as with royalty), allow your hands to slide down the sides of your body.

Electronic Communications

The Telephone

It is important to remember good manners when you are using the telephone. Here are a few guidelines to follow:

- Listen for a second before dialing. Someone may be using the phone in another room.

- Answer the telephone with a pleasant "Hello," not "Yeah."

- Remember that sound is amplified (made louder) when you use the phone. Therefore, don't eat, drink or chew gum when you are talking on the telephone.

- When you answer the phone and the call is for someone else, tell the caller that you will get that person, then put the phone down GENTLY and go tell the other person. Don't just stand by the phone and yell! *Remember–telephones amplify sounds!*

- If the person receiving the call is not there, be sure to take a message. Get the numbers and message information correct. It's a good idea to ask the caller to repeat it if you're not sure. Then be sure to deliver the message.

- When dialing, if you dial a wrong number, you should say, "I'm sorry, I have a wrong number," and hang up.

- When you call a friend and someone else answers, give your name to the person answering. For example: "This is Justin Jones. May I please speak to Adam."

- If you sneeze, cough or clear your throat while you are talking on the telephone, you should cover the mouthpiece and say, "Excuse me." Again remember that the sound is amplified in the other person's ear and makes it seem as though you are sneezing in his or her face.

- Do discuss with your family how much personal (private) and family information to give out over the phone. *Never* tell a stranger on the phone that you are alone.

- Do discuss family rules or likes and dislikes about telephone use in the family. This includes timing of calls and their length of time. Ask your friends about their family rules about the phone. They may be different than yours.

- You should have an understanding with your parents or with the adult in charge of how late at night you may use the telephone and receive telephone calls. Tell your friends your time limit, and also ask your friends about their time limits.

- Unless it's very important, it is rude to call a friend early in the morning when everyone is trying to get off to school or work. It is also rude to call a friend during their dinner time.

- Never use the telephone in someone else's house without first asking permission. Then make the call very brief. Be sure to ask if you must make a long distance charge. In some places, it is common to have a telephone charge of some kind on every call.

- When you use a public or pay phone, be brief if someone else is waiting to use the same phone.

Telephone Answering Machines

- When you leave a message on an answering machine, be sure to speak clearly and give your phone number (so your call may be returned) slowly and clearly. You may want to repeat your number.

- Don't leave a silly message on someone's answering machine. This indicates thoughtlessness and immaturity no matter what age you are or how funny you think the message may be.

- Be cautious about how much personal and family information you leave on an answering machine.

- Don't record a silly or foolish message on your own home answering machine.

Computer-Fax

Even though you cannot be seen or your voice heard, the message that you send on a fax machine or a computer also sends a mental picture of you. Therefore, thoughtfulness, courtesy and good manners are always important.

The growth of electronic communication usage requires some rules beneficial to all.

Generally acceptable guidelines for electronic communications:

1. Never use profanity, obscenity, or other language that may be offensive to another user.
2. Never post someone else's communications without the author's prior consent.
3. Copying commercial software is in violation of copyright laws.
4. Never use the network for illegal activity.

Electronic communications etiquette:

1. Make your "subject line" as descriptive as possible.
2. Compose e-mail and bulletins off line in order to reduce unnecessary network traffic.
3. Always include a salutation before your message: "Dear John . . ."
4. Always sign your name or pseudonym (code name). If possible, include your e-mail address.
5. Always restate or describe the question that you are answering or the issue on which you are commenting.
6. Always acknowledge that you have received a document or file someone has sent you.
7. Check your e-mail once or twice a week, if you are expecting replies.
8. Delete e-mail once you have read it.
9. Don't send personal messages on conferences, bulletin boards, or digests.
10. Don't expect an answer in less than 2-3 days.
11. When sending a file, give as much information as possible: length, type, contents.

12. Conference and bulletin-board messages are "showcases" for all to read. Proofread and edit all messages.

13. Don't be vulgar or offensive. Electronic text allows no context clues to convey shades of irony, sarcasm, or harmless humor.

14. Don't publicly criticize (or "flame") other network users.

15. Protect others' privacy.

16. Protect your own privacy. Most exchanges on the Internet are between strangers. Any overly personal suggestions such as to send your picture or to meet some place should immediately be discussed with your parents or caregiver.

17. Don't upload or download software illegally. It is a serious federal crime.

18. Don't access services illegally.

19. Be careful not to spread computer viruses. Always check downloaded files.

Internet Golden Rule
"Censor Yourself–Not Others"

Dining Table Manners

Most table manners are simple, sensible guidelines for behaving and eating to avoid being "gross" while you are eating. As you grow older you will realize that how you eat, how you behave, the conversation at the table, how you look, and the table setting are all a part of what adults refer to as enjoyable dining.

We'll start out with a few simple rules for dining anywhere, and then discuss more detailed dining. The more you practice these simple rules, the more confident you will feel in any dining situation.

Simple Table Rules

- Come to the dining table as neat and clean as possible. (You don't have to be reminded to *always* wash your hands before eating!)

- Be pleasant and courteous at the table.

- *Never* talk with food in your mouth.

- Chew with your mouth closed. No one wants to see what you are chewing.

- You should never say anything "gross" even though you think it's very funny. To do so makes you seem uncouth. (Uncouth means strange, awkward, rude, boorish, or untrained.)

- You should never do anything repulsive at the table such as a "loud burp." If a burp happens accidently, just say "excuse me." If this happens to someone else, ignore it. Don't laugh.

- *Always* keep your elbows off the table.

- *Never* lean your chair back on its two back legs. Not only is it an uncouth and rude thing to do, but you might break the chair, not to mention the risk of injury!

Table Tips: Good Things to Know at the Table

- Wait until the host or hostess indicates the meal is ready before going to the table.

- The host or hostess will indicate in which chair you should sit. Never say, "Oh, I don't want to sit there." You will upset the seating plan and it will make the person by whom you were supposed to sit feel embarrassed or hurt. Good manners include thoughtfulness!

- Stand behind your chair until the hostess indicates you should be seated.

- Get into the chair from the right. If everyone does this, it saves confusion. If others use either side of the chair, then seat yourself with the least confusion possible.

- If you are a boy, you should first help slide the chair in for the girl who is on your right. Then turn to the girl or woman on your left. If she has been helped, seat yourself. If she has not been helped, try to help her finish sliding in her chair.

- Practice this on your mom, stepmom, or sister. They'll

be impressed! When you are very small, it's more of a thoughtful gesture but, as you grow, you learn to be of real help. Also, the gesture becomes a habit. If a person is old or feeble, they may also need your help, so this action becomes more than just a courtesy.

- Ask an adult to show you how he slides a chair in for the women and then you can take turns.

- After everyone is seated at the table, *before* you put your napkin in your lap, look at your host or hostess and wait to see if there will be a "blessing" of the food. This is often called "a grace." If there is one, listen quietly with your head slightly bowed and your hands in your lap.

- Wait until the host or hostess (at home your mother is usually the hostess) takes the napkin to put in his or her lap, then put your napkin in your lap. (To learn more about this, see Napkin section, page 54.)

- Wait for the hostess or host to pick up a fork to start eating before you pick up your fork and start eating.

- At the table it's a good idea to slow down your movements and not talk with your hands to avoid embarrassing accidents. Also, never wave your spoon or fork (with or without food attached) in the air when you are talking.

- To take a big drink of something and go "Ahhhh" is in the same category as a big burp. It's uncouth and rude—so don't.

- Sit up straight while you are at the table. To lean way over on the table and put your arm around your plate gives the impression that you are trying to sleep on the table.

- When eating with a fork or spoon, only take the amount you can eat at one time. When you put a bite of food into your mouth, hold your lips closed around the fork or spoon so the food is cleaned off of your fork or spoon before you remove it from your mouth. It's tempting to put a heaping spoonful of ice cream into your mouth and bring the spoon back out with some of the ice cream still on the spoon, but don't. This is ugly to see and a rude thing to do.

Where Do Your Hands Go?

- There was a time when we kept our hands folded gracefully in our laps. But in today's life we have no reason to keep hands below the table. You may keep your *wrists* resting on the table edge, not elbows on the table. (We in the United States are the only ones in the world who often keep our hands under the table while we are eating.)

- When you cut your food, your elbows should not "fly out" like chicken wings from your body. (Practice by putting a thin book under each arm and keep them there while you cut your food. It's kind of silly, but it helps you know how much your arms and elbows do stick out.)

- You should prepare no more than two bites at a time. Cut two (no more than three) pieces of meat or other foods at one time. If you are younger and can't manage the knife yet, don't worry; just enjoy having someone cut your food. One of these days you'll be cutting your own; then you will know just what to do.

- Take small bites so that you don't have to open your mouth so wide to put food in. It's easier to chew small bites with your mouth closed and you can chew your food more completely. Also you can swallow sooner to be able to take part in the conversation at the table or to answer a question if you don't have such a big bite to chew.

- Even if you are very hungry, don't "shovel" your food into your mouth. Take your time. Chew each bite entirely—swallow it before you take another bite.

- Don't stir and "mix up" the different foods on your plate.

- Try some of everything that is served to you whether you think you will like it or not. Never say, "I don't want any." Try it—you might like it! If you truly don't like it or you have an allergy, leave it on your plate. Of course, at home you may discuss your dislikes with your parent.

- Once silverware is used it must never be returned to the table. Put it on the proper plate or saucer. (To learn more about silverware, see Ways of Eating, page 57.)

- Do not play with the silverware or use it to drum on the table.

- If you drop a piece of silverware, ask the hostess for another one. Leave the one you dropped until after the meal; then pick it up when you are leaving the table. In a restaurant ask the waiter for another one. Leave the dropped piece where it is, and the waiter will pick it up.

- If you ask the waiter for something, do remember the word "Please."

- You don't have to eat everything on your plate. At the same time, don't announce "I'm full." Just sit quietly.

- When you are finished, leave your plate where it is. Don't push your plate back from the edge of the table toward the middle of the table.

- Never stack your dishes in front of you, even if you are clearing your own plate.

- Wait for the host or hostess to start eating his or her dessert before you start to eat yours.

- If the meal is finished and adults are still talking and drinking coffee or tea, it is perfectly proper to ask, "May I please be excused?" However, if you are at the table at a friend's party, you must stay at the table until the guest of honor is finished and the host or hostess indicates that all of you may leave the table.

- When everyone has finished the meal and you are leaving the table, put your napkin back on the table on the left side of your plate no matter where you found it when you sat down. Do not refold your napkin.

Being Served by a Waiter

- The waiter will serve you from the left. Dishes will be removed from the right.

- When you are served from a bowl with a spoon, serve yourself only reasonable helpings. You don't want to appear to be a glutton (a pig), even if you are starved.

- If you are being served from a platter that has both a large spoon and a fork, slightly turn to your left, toward the tray, pick up the serving spoon in your right hand and the fork in your left hand. Use the spoon to take up the food and the fork to steady it as you transfer the food to your plate. Don't hurry. Take your time. Then, replace the fork and spoon, side by side, on the serving platter. Do remember to keep the handles clear of food.

- Take what's nearest you and do not hunt around for your favorite piece.

- When something is served that you don't like, take a small amount. This is more courteous than saying "No thank you."

- It is not necessary to thank the waiter or any other person who is serving you every time you are served. If you are offered a second helping, then a "Yes, please" or Yes, thank you" is pleasant.

- However, you do need to say "No, thank you" when you refuse something or a second helping.

Food and Your Teeth

- Braces on your teeth: At sometime or another, many of you have to wear braces on your teeth. If food gets lodged in your teeth or "braces" and you can't get it out with your tongue, do *not* sit at the table and pick at it with a fingernail or a toothpick. Excuse yourself and go to the bathroom and take care of the problem. When you are wearing braces, it is wise to carry a toothbrush or a 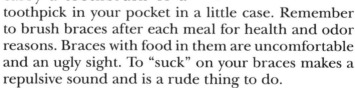 toothpick in your pocket in a little case. Remember to brush braces after each meal for health and odor reasons. Braces with food in them are uncomfortable and an ugly sight. To "suck" on your braces makes a repulsive sound and is a rude thing to do.

- Toothpicks: Toothpicks are in the same category as dental floss and toothbrushes for cleaning the teeth: they all belong in the bathroom and should only be used in the bathroom.

Toasting: Bon Appetit, Skoal, Buen Provecho

- A "toast" is a drink to the health of a person. A "toast" honors a person or commemorates an event. Toasting is something that you should know about because it's done often, particularly on special occasions. Generally, it's the host or hostess who proposes the first toast. A toast can be made for any special reason, including honoring the guest of honor, recognizing a birthday, congratulating someone who has made the honor roll or "toasting" to everyone's good health.

- At a large dinner, everyone stands for the toast *except* the person who is being toasted.

- At a small dinner party, such as in a home, only the person making the toast stands. If the number at the table is small, such as six or less, all may remain seated, including the person proposing the toast.

- After the toast is said, the guests take a drink from their wine or champagne glasses.

- The person being toasted never drinks to himself.

- Until you are older, of course, you probably won't be drinking wine or champagne. Hopefully, the hostess was thoughtful enough to have a glass of juice, soda or milk at your place. Use any one of these glasses to raise and take a sip after the toast. If you have only water, it is permissible to use that. (However, when you are "older," you should know that to drink a toast to someone with water, when you have a wine glass, is a superstition thought of as bad luck and therefore an insult.)

- When "toasting" you do not need to "clink" glasses around the table. All that is necessary for you to do is to lift your glass, about chin high, in front of you. In fact, sometimes to clink glasses around the table can be awkward.

- To "clink" glasses is a nice gesture that says, "Here's to you," "*Bon appetit*," "*Skoal*," "*Salud*" or "*Buen Provecho.*" "Clinking glasses" is generally done by a small group at the table, two or six. More than six becomes a little clumsy.

- *Bon Appetit*—French meaning "good appetite" or "eat well." *Skoal* is a Scandanavian word meaning "to your good health" or "may you prosper." *Salud* is a Spanish word meaning "health" or "to your good health." *Buen Provecho* is a Spanish toast meaning "Enjoy your meal."

- Even at a young age, you can practice toasts at home so that, when you become an adult, you will already have the social asset of knowing how to give and receive toasts. You might start with giving a toast to your parent's good cooking, or your sibling's good grades.

- Practice proposing toasts at home and you will have the "know-how" when you are at a party in a home or at a celebration in a restaurant.

Typical Place Settings

This place setting tells you that soup will be served because there is a soup spoon (#1). The salad will be served next because the salad fork (#2) is on the outside. The main course will be served next (#3). Bread will be served. There is a bread and butter plate (#4).

Formal Place Settings

These are typical place settings for party dinners at home and in most nice restaurants today. The place setting includes a lot of silverware, but with a little practice, you'll know when to use each piece.

1. Napkin—generally to the left of your plate and forks. It may be placed in your plate or in any attractive place that your hostess wishes to put it. See page 54 for napkin etiquette.

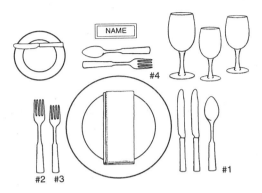

This place setting tells you that soup (#1) will be served first; next, your entrée (main course) (#2); your salad after the main course (#3). How do you know this? By seeing and using your utensils in their order from the outside toward the plate. You know dessert will be served because a salad fork and spoon are above the plate (#4). Three or four glasses might hold water, milk, soda, juice, or several different wines for adults. If the glasses will not be used, the waiter will remove them.

This place setting tells you that bread (#1) and soup will be served (#2). Next will be the fish course (#3). The entrée will be served next (#4). The salad course will be served next, and the utensils will be brought at that time. Finger bowls may or may not be brought. Silverware for dessert will be presented when dessert is served.

2. Salad plate or bread and butter plate—bread and butter plate is smaller than a salad plate. If it is a bread and butter plate, it will probably have a butter knife on it. The knife blade will be turned toward the center of the plate. After the knife is used, return it to this position on the bread and butter plate. The salad plate is larger than the bread and butter plate and placed on the table in the same position above and slightly to the left of the entrée plate. It has no knife on it. Generally both plates are not placed on the table at the same time. Often the salad plate already has salad on it. If you serve yourself salad, place your salad on this plate. Also your roll and butter or jam may be placed on your salad plate.

3. Dinner plate—(entrée plate)—for the main course.

4. Salad fork—for salad or for dessert. The tines are shorter than the dinner fork and placed on the left of the entrée plate. When it is to be used for dessert it is placed at the top of the entrée plate with or without a spoon.

5. Dinner fork—(entrée fork)—for the main course is placed on the left side of the entrée plate.

6. Dinner knife—(entrée knife)—for meat and anything else that needs to be cut that is served on the main course plate. It is placed on the right side of the entrée plate.

7. Teaspoon—to stir coffee or tea. Also used for dessert or for almost anything that needs to be eaten with a spoon. It is placed to the right of the entrée plate on the right side of the knife or at the top of the entrée plate if it is to be used for dessert.

8. Soup spoon—is for soup or desserts. It is placed to the right of the entrée plate or at the top of the entrée plate if it is to be used for dessert.

9. Water glass—sometimes referred to as a water goblet. A "tumbler" is a glass with a flat bottom and straight up and down sides and is most often used for the water or milk glass. Its placement is above and on the right side of the plate, above the dinner knife.

10. Wine glass—until you are an adult, your hostess might put milk, juice, or soda in this glass. Its placement is above the dinner plate on the right side of the water goblet.

11. Place card—if a place card with your name on it is used at a dinner party or birthday party, it would generally be placed directly above your plate.

12. Finger bowl—a small bowl filled about a third full with water. The finger bowl will be brought to you after the main course, so it wouldn't be placed on the table before the meal. Sometimes there is a flower or a thin slice of lemon floating in the water. They are only for decoration so don't try to eat them! (See below.)

Finger Bowls

The dessert fork and spoon will be served to you on a plate with a small bowl of water sitting on a doily. Dip your fingertips into the bowl, *one hand at a time*, and dry them on your napkin.

Then take both hands, one on each side, grasping the doily and bowl, placing them to the left and above where your dessert fork will go (about

where your salad plate was). Then, with both hands at the same time, palce the dessert fork on the left side and the spoon on the right of the dessert plate. Dessert will be served and put on this plate.

If a finger bowl is brought to you and there is no silverware on the little plate, it might mean that there is no dessert, so don't remove the bowl from the plate unless your hostess removes hers and places it properly. Then, of course, follow her movements. Also, the finger bowl can be brought at the end of the meal. If so, leave it on your little plate. Follow the lead of your host or hostess.

If there is to be a dessert, the silverware needed and the dessert will be served to you.

Informal Place Settings

The main difference between the table place settings for a formal dinner and informal dinner is the number of pieces of silverware, plates and glasses used on the table.

The typical informal place setting would include (see the following illustration #1):

Informal place setting #1

- Napkin—to the left of your plate and fork. It may be folded in a fancy shape, placed in your glass, or any attractive place your hostess wishes to put it.
- Dinner fork (entrée fork)
- Dinner knife (entrée knife)
- Teaspoon
- A glass
- With or without a teaspoon and salad fork for dessert at the top of the plate.

If a salad were to be served then you could have a salad plate and a salad fork added to the place setting. The salad fork would be to the left of your dinner fork. The salad plate would be at the top left of your dinner plate. (See the following illustration #2.)

Dessert Fork and Spoon

Informal place setting #2

When you see a salad fork or a spoon or both at the top of your plate, they are meant to be used for dessert. If there is only a bread and butter plate, or no bread and butter plate, your salad will probably be served on your main course dinner plate. You should use your dinner fork for the salad. If you have a salad on a salad plate you will have a fork for salad on your left. Just remember that the salad fork at the top of the plate is meant for dessert.

Chopsticks

Japanese, Chinese, Korean, Thai, Vietnamese and other Asian food restaurants have become popular in the United States. Eating Asian foods with a knife, fork and spoon is certainly proper, but it is not as much fun as eating them with chopsticks. Someone who knows how to use chopsticks can show you the proper way to eat with them, or the waiter at the restaurant can show you how to use them.. Try it! It is a nice experience to be able to master chopsticks. Chopsticks can be used at home too. Once chopsticks are used, they should be placed on your bowl or chopstick holders, not back on the linen or table.

Table Decorations

Flowers on the table are appropriate anytime—breakfast, lunch or dinner. They lend a gentle, lovely and caring touch. They should be low enough that people are able to see each other across the table.

Candles are appropriate and festive for dinner. They are not appropriate at lunch or a brunch.

Napkins

Napkin rings should be used strictly for decoration on the napkin and table. Once your napkin is taken out of the napkin ring and used, don't put the napkin back in the ring. In days long past, napkin rings were used by the family because napkins were re-used before they were washed. Each person generally had their own identifying napkin ring. Today cloth napkins are washed after each use.

Your napkin will generally be either on your plate or on the table to your left and left of your forks. Sometimes napkins are folded in fancy shapes and placed in other places. No matter how napkins are folded or where they are placed you handle them in the same way.

- Dinner napkins are large. Leave folded in half. When you put your napkin in your lap, the folded edge goes toward your body. If you have a small napkin, fold it out flat over your lap. The idea of a napkin is to catch any food that accidentally drops.

- Your napkin belongs in your lap during the entire meal. If, for some important reason, you have to leave the table during the meal, just say, "Excuse me." Push your chair back carefully, and leave the table as quietly as possible. But put your napkin ON YOUR CHAIR, not on the table. When you return to the table, put your napkin back in your lap.

- Your napkin should be used to blot your mouth. It is not to be used as a handkerchief. If you do get caught with a sneeze that comes on so quickly that you can't get to your tissue or handkerchief, then, by all means, use the napkin to cover your nose and mouth. That's better than nothing. But NEVER blow your nose into the napkin, even if it is a paper napkin. If you need a tissue or handkerchief, excuse yourself from the table. Blow your nose, then return to the table.

- Before you drink from a glass or cup, you can pat (not rub) your mouth with your napkin to keep food from sticking to the rim of the glass when you drink.

- Generally, only babies or people with eating difficulties wear napkins tucked in at the neck.

- When you return to the buffet table between courses of a meal served buffet style, leave your napkin in your chair.

- At the end of the meal when everyone has finished the meal and all of you are leaving the table, place the used napkin back on the table unfolded on the left side of your place setting.

Ways of Eating

There are two ways to use your silverware. They are both acceptable and appropriate. One is called the "Continental Method" and the other is called the "United States Method," commonly known as the "Zig-Zag Method." We in the United States are the only people in the world who use the "zig-zag" way of eating. More and more people in the United States are using the "Continental Method" because it's easier and makes sense.

When cutting your food, hold your knife and fork the same way for both Continental and Zig-Zag methods of eating.

Zig-Zag Method of Using a Knife and Fork

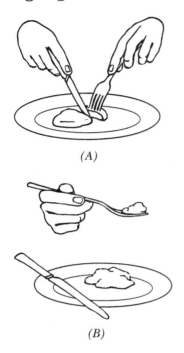

(A)

(B)

With the Zig-Zag Method you hold your fork in your left hand and cut your food with a knife in your right hand (illustration A). Then you put the knife across the top right side of your plate (B) with the blade toward the plate center. The fork is moved to the right hand for eating. The left hand can rest in your lap or your *wrist* may rest on the table edge. (You *never* rest the knife handle on the table and the blade on the plate.) This is called "gang planking" (C). Put your fork in your right hand and carry your food to your mouth with the right hand. When you are finished, place your knife and fork side by side with tines up in the lower righthand fourth of the plate about the four o'clock position (D). This also signals to the waiter that you are finished.

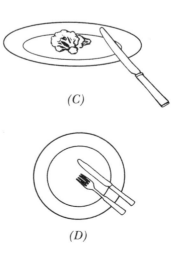

(C)

(D)

Continental Method of Using a Knife and Fork

- To use the Continental Method of eating, put your fork in your left hand and your knife in your right hand and cut your food just the way you do in the Zig-Zag Method. Then keep your fork in your left hand with the tines down and carry your food to your mouth. This works well when the tines of your fork are in meats and solid foods.

- Soft foods are gently mashed on the back of the fork (tines down), and then put in your mouth. Keep your knife in your right hand while you put the food in your mouth. You may rest your wrists on the table edge or rest your knife and fork on your plate while you are chewing. The knife and fork are held this way all through your meal.

- If you put your knife and fork down during the meal, place them in an upside-down "V" on your plate with the fork tines down (illustration E below), and knife blade toward the center of the plate. Salad utensils are also used in this manner. Utensils placed at the

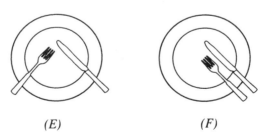

(E)   *(F)*

four o'clock position with the fork tines down and the knife blade toward the fork on the left signals that you are finished (F).

- When desserts are served, they are eaten with the spoon and fork that were placed at the top of your dinner plate (illustrations 1 & 2, pp. 52-53). For des-

sert, put the spoon in your
right hand and the fork in
your left hand. Gently scoop
the spoon and hold the fork
with tines down. Use the fork
to steady the food while you
use the spoon (illustration
G).

(G)

- Use the spoon and fork for
  pie and ice cream, or cake
  and ice cream.

- Pie or cake is eaten with a fork in the right hand,
  spoon in the left; use the spoon as a pusher.

- Ice cream, puddings and custards are eaten with a
  spoon only.

- Cut-up fruit or berries are eaten with a spoon in the
  right hand and a fork in the left hand with tines down
  or with the spoon only.

- If you don't already use the Continental Method of
  eating, you should seriously consider asking your parents or person in charge to introduce you to this style
  of eating because, not only is it more efficient, qui-
  eter and easier, but when you grow up and travel to
  other countries, you will have already mastered this
  method of eating. Therefore you won't feel so awkward or out of place. Try it. It is fun.

Eating with the Fish Knife and Fork

With the tines down, the fish fork is held in the left
hand. Hold the fish knife like a pencil in the right hand.
The fork is held in the left hand and the knife is used to
cut and as a pusher. Mash the fish on the back of the
tines-down fork and put the bite into your mouth using
the Continental Method of eating. In the United States

today, the fish fork and knife are not generally used unless the service is formal. Otherwise use your regular silverware in your preferred method of eating.

When you go to a restaurant, it should be an en-

joyable outing for everyone. Use your best manners. If you have been practicing your manners and how to use different utensils at home, they will seem natural and comfortable. It will be easier for you to enjoy your surroundings and the conversation if you know what to do and what is expected of you.

Never hold your fork with a "fist" when you are cutting a piece of meat or any other food.

How to Eat Different Foods

These are the guidelines for eating foods that can give you a problem at some time or another. If you know the way they are easiest to eat, and if you know the most acceptable way to eat them, then they should give you no problem. Eat and enjoy!

Artichokes

- Artichokes are a finger food *and* a knife and fork food. The leaves are pulled off, one at a time, with your fingers. While still holding the leaf in your fingers, the "fat" end should be dipped in the little individual dish of sauce. Then put your teeth over the "fat" part  and strip the "fat" part off with your teeth. Put the remaining leaf on the plate beside the artichoke. If there isn't much room on that plate, put the leaf on your bread and butter plate. If there is no bread and butter plate, put the leaf on your salad plate.

- When you've pulled all of the leaves off, you'll see the heart, or middle, left. This is called the "choke."

Cut the "choke" loose from the bottom with your knife. Then cut the "choke" into small pieces. Using your fork, dip the pieces in the little sauce dish and eat them. It's a lot of work for not much food, but it's fun to know how to eat artichokes properly when they are served. This is a food that's good to practice eating at home.

Asparagus

Asparagus should be eaten with a fork. Generally, hot asparagus has butter or a sauce on it, and it would be messy to eat with your fingers. The soft top part can be cut with the edge of the fork. The more firm part is cut into bite-size pieces with a knife, then put into your mouth with a fork. If asparagus is served as a cold-pickled "hors d'oeuvre finger food," then it can be eaten with your fingers.

Bacon

Even though it's tempting to do so, don't eat bacon with your fingers. Bacon should be eaten with a knife and fork. When bacon is soft, there is no problem cutting it. When bacon is crisp, it sometimes flies all over the table when you cut it, even though you are trying to be careful. This is embarrassing and annoying. If you are in a restaurant or are someone's guest, you haven't much choice but to use your knife and fork. At home, you can let your conscience be your guide and probably use your fingers for crisp bacon.

Baked Potatoes

For a small child, it is proper to scoop out the contents of a baked potato and mash it up with butter. It is *not* proper for adults to do this, so it is up to you to decide your stage of "growing up." If you wish to eat only the potato part, that's okay, just eat it out of the skin. If you wish to eat the skin also, cut it with your knife and fork into small bites. It is proper to eat the skin. It is also proper to put condiments (butter, bacon bits, cheese, whatever is to your liking) on your baked potato.

Bread and Butter

- Bread, butter and roll go on the bread and butter plate. So does jam or jelly if you intend to put the jam on your roll or bread.

- Break off small bite-size pieces from your roll or bread. Breaking and buttering are done while you hold the roll or bread pieces either rested on the bread plate or low over the plate and almost on the plate to keep crumbs from flying over the table. Butter the pieces one bite at a time.

- Use the small butter knife to butter each bite as it is eaten. Do not butter the whole roll or all of the pieces at one time.

- Jam is put on roll and bread pieces the same way as butter is put on pieces. One bite at a time with your butter knife. If there is no butter knife use your dinner knife.

- Sticky buns and other sweet rolls should be cut or pulled apart into quarters or small pieces and eaten the same way as your bread and rolls. If they are especially sticky or have a frosting of some sort on them, you may want to use your fork to eat them.

- If there is butter already on your bread and butter plate and no serving plate of butter on the table, do not ask for more butter. The butter on the plate is meant only for your bread or roll—not for your baked potato or vegetables.

- When you are taking butter from a plate that is being passed, use the knife that is on the butter plate, not your dinner knife or your salad knife. If there is no butter knife, then use an unused knife from your place setting.

- If there is no bread and butter plate, use the edge of your salad plate for your butter and your bread or roll. If there is no salad plate, then use the edge of your entrée plate (main meal plate) on which to put your butter.

Candies and Nuts at the Table

Most often when you are served candies for dessert, they will have the little frilly papers under them. Pick up the paper with the candy. Leave the candy in the paper cup and place it on the tablecloth next to your plate until you are ready to eat it. Then just pick up the candy with your fingers. If there is no paper under the candies, put them on your plate.

When nuts are served at the table, they will probably be passed in a small bowl with a spoon. Use the spoon to place the nuts on your dessert plate, not on the tablecloth or place mat.

Catsup and Mustard

We in the United States are great condiment eaters. (*Condiment*—kon-do-ment, something used to give flavor and relish to foods, like catsup and mustard.) Relish is something to add flavor and taste. Catsup and mustard are probably the most used of all condiments.

- At home or in a restaurant, mustard and catsup should be put on your plate and then put on your hamburgers or hot dogs.

- At a picnic, it is okay to put mustard and catsup directly on your hot dogs or hamburgers that are in a bun.

- If you use catsup on your French fries, use your fork to cut the French fries, and then neatly dip in the catsup each bite of French fries that is on your fork. If you don't have a fork, put the catsup on your plate, use your fingers for the French fries and dip them neatly in your catsup.

- Catsup is dispensed in many different containers: the pump, the squeeze bottle or a jar with a little spoon. The most common way to dispense catsup is to pour it directly from its own bottle. Simply lift the bottle and hold it at an angle over the place on your plate in which you wish the catsup to be poured.

What do you do when the catsup doesn't pour, doesn't pour, doesn't pour, no matter how carefully you gently shake the bottle? First, hope that much more than what you want doesn't "splat" out all over everything on your plate! Sometimes holding the bottle at an angle and gently tapping on the underneath side of the bottle with your finger will encourage the catsup to come out.

If it still doesn't come out, you might carefully hold the bottle on its side, use a clean, unused knife and *cautiously*, using the tip of the knife blade, unclog the catsup bottle at the top of the neck. Try tipping the bottle up again and hope it doesn't "burble" out a big blob! Good luck!

- Mustard is generally in a squeeze bottle, a bottle with a pump, a little jar with a spatula or a spoon. Squeeze the squeeze bottle carefully, pump the pump carefully or use the spoon to put the mustard on your food. When mustard is put on a hot dog in a hot dog bun, it may be put on the full length of the hot dog.

- In many of the fast-food restaurants today, mustard and catsup are given to you in little foil packets. Tear open the packet and squeeze the mustard or catsup directly on to your food. Fast-food restaurants are considered casual.

Caviar

Caviar is a rare delicacy. Caviar is a fancy name for fish eggs. Caviar is usually served in a small crystal bowl set in ice with a small spoon in it. Little pieces of toast or crackers will be served with the caviar. Put one spoonful of the caviar (never more than one) on your bread and butter plate or salad plate. Put the caviar on the pieces of toast or crackers with a little knife like a bread and butter knife. (The knife will be on the table.) If there is no little knife, use your dinner knife. If you are at a party and are not sitting at the table, use the little spoon that is in the caviar dish to put the caviar on the toast or crackers.

Celery, Olives, Radishes, Carrot Sticks, Etc.

When you sit down to dinner, there is often a plate of carrot sticks, celery sticks, olives, pickled onions, radishes, and other small tidbits already on the table or served soon after you are seated. They may be passed by the waiter or they may be passed family style. Take some of whichever you wish and put them on your bread and butter plate. Whatever you take always put it onto your plate first—never directly into your mouth from the tray.

Cherry Tomatoes

Often cherry tomatoes are served whole and

unpeeled in salads. They can be "little rascals." They can shoot off the plate when you try to put your fork into them. If they are too large to eat in one bite, they must be cut in half. To do that can be tricky but not if you put your knife behind, or to the side of, the tomato and steady it so it won't roll away while you put your fork tines into the tomato. Then calmly slice the tomato in half with your knife.

Chicken

Chicken, cooked in many ways, is an all-time favorite in the United States and maybe the world over. Fried chicken is traditional and the most favorite of all. At picnics, barbecues, or any casual outdoor gathering, fried chicken is eaten with your fingers. Just remember not to "gnaw" on the bones, or lick your fingers, and remember to wipe your face often.

At the family dinner table, at dinner parties, and at restaurants, chicken should be eaten with a knife and fork. It helps your confidence to practice this as soon as you are old enough to use a knife and fork.

Clams (Steamed)

When you are served steamed clams, they will be in a bowl. The shell will be open. Hold the shell in one hand, over your bowl. With your fork in the other hand, lift out the clam. Dip the clam into the broth or butter that is served with it in a small individual bowl. Put the whole clam in your mouth.

- Put the shell on the plate that is under the bowl or in any dish that might be provided for the shells.

- Steaming opens the shell of good clams. If a clam shell is not open, never "pry" it open because if the shell is not open, the clam is probably NOT GOOD. (Clams are not usually served at dress-up dinner parties.)

Cookies

- Cookies are taken from the serving tray with your fingers. Take one at a time no matter how small they might be. The cookie is placed on your plate and the tray passed on before you take a bite of your cookie. If the cookie is large, break it in two with your fingers. If the cookie is small, it doesn't need to be broken.

- When cookies are served with ice cream or a sauce of fruit, the cookie is put on the edge of the dessert plate. If you have no dessert plate, then put it on the tablecloth.

- If it is a cookie with frosting, your hostess will give you some kind of dessert plate.

Consommé

- Consommé is a clear broth. It may be served in a cup. If consommé is served in a cup, you may drink from the cup; but watch your host or hostess to see what he or she does. If consommé is served in a bowl (with no handles) always use a spoon.

- Cream soups are always eaten with a spoon no matter how they are served.

Corn on the Cob

- Corn on the cob is served only at informal meals because it is so messy and difficult to eat.

- You may put whatever is offered to you (butter, salt, etc.) on your ear of corn.
- If you use butter and salt, butter only a few rows of your corn at a time.
- Hold the cob firmly by the fingers of both hands. Sometimes there are little cob holders in each end of the corn cob you can hold on to. If there are no cob holders, hold the cob firmly with the fingers of both hands.
- Bite the corn from the cob with a scraping motion with your teeth.
- Never cut corn off the cob at the table.
- If kernels do get caught in your teeth, excuse yourself and go to the bathroom to pick your teeth. Don't pick your teeth at the table.

Crab

Ask your parent or caregiver to crack your crab. In a restaurant you or your host or hostess may ask your waiter or waitress to crack it for you. After it is cracked, you use a small pick provided for you to remove the crab meat from its shell. Place the crab meat on your plate and eat it with a fork.

Crackers

Crackers should *never* be crumbled in your soup. Take one or two crackers at a time when they are passed. Depending on their size, bite into them if they are small or break them with your fingers and put part of them on your plate if they are large.

Oyster crackers are little round crackers. They will be served in a bowl with a large spoon. Take a spoonful and put them on your bread and butter plate or on the plate that's under your soup bowl. Then take one or two at a time in your fingers, and put them in your soup.

Fish Bones

Fish bones can be dangerous. Any fish bone in your mouth should be removed with your thumb and forefinger ANYTIME, ANYPLACE.

Small fish, such as trout, are often cleaned, fried and served whole. To eat the whole fish, cut the head off first, then hold the fish firmly with your fork. Cut the fish open with your knife and open the fish out flat. The fish bones can generally be pulled out with fingers or fork. Put the bones on the edge of your plate. BE VERY CAREFUL of the bones. Until you are older you might want to ask for help with this kind of fish dish.

French Fries

- In the United States, French fries are thought of as a casual food, sort of like potato chips. It's acceptable to eat French fries with your fingers or fork, even though they are most often dipped into catsup (See page 66—Catsup).

- Sometimes French fries are covered with a gravy or sauce. Then, of course, they must be eaten with a fork.

Frog Legs and Small Game Birds

Frog legs and game birds such as quail, squab or Cornish game hens are not often served. However, if you are served one and don't know what to do with it, it can present quite a dilemma, even for adults. These small foods are slippery and difficult to control on the plate. Carefully, cut off as much meat as you can with your knife and fork and eat it with your fork. Then, as gracefully as possible, with your fingers, you may pick up the little bones and, without seeming to "gnaw," do the best you can. You must remember to often pat your face with your napkin. The host or hostess will generally be thoughtful enough to indicate that you can use your fingers.

Fruit

- Fruit can be eaten with a fork or a spoon. Fruit may be served in many ways for salads or desserts. The utensil that is used to eat them depends on how the fruit is served. For example, grapefruit cut in half and left in the rind is eaten with a spoon, but grapefruit segments in a salad are eaten with a fork.
- The best plan in the case of fruit is to follow your host or hostess's actions.

Garnishes

- It is okay to eat the "garnishes" on your plate. Garnishes are those little pieces of parsley, lemon and orange that are put on your plates to make them look more attractive.
- Sometimes a slice or wedge of lemon on your plate is meant to be squeezed on your fish or other food. Squeeze it with one hand while you cup your other hand over it. That way it won't squirt on someone or on the table. Sometimes these slices of lemon are covered with a small piece of fine meshed cloth. Leave the cloth on the lemon and squeeze them the same way with your hand.

Hors d'Oeuvres

- *Hors d'oeuvres* is generally pronounced like "or-durvs." The name simply means a relish or light food served before a meal. Hors d'oeuvres can be peanuts in a dish, cheese and crackers, fresh vegetables cut in small pieces to be dipped in a dip, or just about anything that is tasty. Hors d'oeuvres are normally served on a table set up just for them.

- You can take a small amount, or one piece, and eat it directly from your fingers.

- If a small plate is provided, then you can take a plate and put one or two pieces of each food that is offered onto your small plate. Carefully take the small plate someplace away from the hors d'oeuvre table to eat the food.

- If there is a dip, you dip your carrot, celery or whatever into the "dip" and then put it on your plate.

- If no plate is provided, dip the carrot, celery or whatever into the dip, step back away from the table and eat the entire piece.

- One thing tempts nearly everyone, but you must not do it—and that is to dip the celery, or whatever, into the dip, eat that part with the dip on it and then re-dip your celery, or whatever, *back into* the dip. (To re-dip the half-eaten celery or whatever, is not only rude and uncouth but would introduce germs from your mouth into the food that was meant to be shared by everyone.)

At one very lovely holiday party, many of the other guests and I watched a young man, who was certainly old enough to know better, stand right by the hors d'oeuvre table, take a piece of celery, dip it into the dip, eat that bite then re-dip the same piece of celery back into the dip. He did this several times. Finally, the hostess saw what was happening and took the entire tray back to the kitchen. His rude and uncouth actions were noticed by everyone, even though no one said anything. The hostess had worked hard to prepare a lovely treat for everyone to share properly and to enjoy, and this young man spoiled it for everyone.

- Sometimes you might put an hors d'oeuvre or two on a little cocktail napkin and eat these with your fingers from the napkin. This method is often difficult to manage even for adults.

- It is proper for you to return to the hors d'oeuvre table several times. It is thoughtful to step back so others can get up to the table. (Even adults are careless about this sometimes.)

Ice Cream and Sherbet

- Knowing whether to use a fork, dessert spoon, or spoon and fork on ice cream depends on how it is served.

- When ice cream or sherbet is served in a small dish, it is eaten with a spoon. When it is served on the same plate with pie or cake, it is eaten with a fork, or a fork and a spoon (see Continental Method, page 59).

- Ice cream cones are not served at a luncheon or dinner party, except for small children's parties.

Jellies

- When jelly that is meant to be eaten with your roll is served, put it on your bread and butter plate. It is put on your roll with the knife, one bite at a time.

- When jelly that is meant to be eaten with meat or fowl is served, put it on your dinner plate. A small amount is put on your fork and eaten with the meat or fowl at the same time. (For example: Often you will be served mint jelly to be eaten with lamb or veal.)

Lobster

Lobster should be prepared in the kitchen so that no further cracking of the shell is necessary. The meat should be held with a fork, cut with a knife into bite-size pieces and then dipped into melted butter or sauce that is served in a small dish with the lobster.

Melons

- Watermelon is generally eaten with a fork.
- Honeydew melon and cantaloupe are eaten with a fork unless they are served uncut in their rind. If they are served in their rind, a spoon is needed.

Olives

If the olives have pits in them, cup your hand and fingers and quietly spit the pit into your fingers. Then put the pit on your salad plate or bread and butter plate.

Pasta

Pasta includes many foods such as macaroni or spaghetti. All pasta dishes are eaten with a fork.

Spaghetti

We all know how slippery good spaghetti is with lots of sauce and how shifty it can be to get it to our mouths. So, while you are growing up and learning to "twine" it properly, a good way to handle spaghetti is to take your fork in one hand and a good-size spoon, like a soup spoon in the other hand, and then put a few strands of spaghetti and sauce on your fork and hold the soup spoon lightly against the spaghetti so it can't get away. Twist your fork and it automatically twines the spaghetti around the fork. Then put the fork and spaghetti in your mouth. Just remember not to take too big of a bite.

- The correct and accepted way to eat spaghetti is to twine a few strands around your fork tines while you hold your fork gently against your plate.

- You may also cut the spaghetti with the side of your fork.

- You might want to lean toward the table a little to help keep the sauce off your clothes. (Lean toward the table, not down over your plate.)

Pizza

Pizza may properly be held in your hand and eaten with your fingers or eaten on a plate with a fork. How you eat it all depends on how messy it is and where you are. Pizza is considered a casual food. It would never be served at a formal dinner party. Just be sure lots of napkins are available.

Potato Chips, Tortilla Chips, Pretzels, Etc.

Chips are eaten with your fingers. Chips are a "noisy food" so chew as quietly as you can! The same "dip only once" rules about dip and vegetables apply to dip and chips. (Please see page 74).

Salad

- Salad can be served before, after or with the entreé (main course).

- Use your salad fork to eat salad. If large pieces cannot be cut with the edge of the salad fork, use a salad knife or your dinner knife. Eat your salad from the salad plate. If salad is served with the main course, there is no salad fork, use your dinner fork. If salad is served on your entrée plate, use your dinner fork.

- Don't transfer your salad from a salad plate to your main course plate.

- When you are finished with a salad fork, place it on the salad plate. (Between bites of salad your fork should be returned to your salad plate.) If you have used a salad knife, place it on the salad plate also, next to the fork with the blade toward the middle of the plate at the 4 o'clock position (see illustration at left).

Salt and Pepper

- It is an insult to the cook if you put salt and pepper on your food before you taste it. This is improper at home or anyplace else.

- Salt and pepper should be passed together and at the same time, even though both are not asked for.

Soup

- Soup is eaten all over the world. In the United States, soup noises are frowned upon. (In some other cultures "slurping sounds" with soup are normal and natural.)

- Cream soup is eaten with a soup spoon. A clear soup may be eaten with a spoon if served in a bowl or drunk from a cup if served in a cup. Follow your host or hostess's lead.

- If your soup is hot, jut stir it a bit, wait a little, and then take small spoonfuls. Don't blow on it.

- Dip your spoon AWAY from you when you are eating soup.

- For a cream soup, it is acceptable to scrape the bottom of your spoon across the edge of your soup bowl as you lift your spoon. It helps to eliminate drips.

- If there are pieces of food in your soup that are too large for one bite, such as vegetables, meat or dumplings, use the side of your spoon to cut the pieces into bite-size. A knife has no place in a soup bowl.

- If your soup is served in a flat soup plate, you should leave your spoon in the plate when you are finished.

- If your soup is served in a cup or a bowl, then you should place your spoon on the plate that is under the bowl when you are finished.

Sauce and Gravy

Sauces that are meant to be eaten with foods on your main course plate should be poured or ladled right onto the food with which they are meant to be eaten. Put the gravy on the potatoes and put the mint sauce on the lamb or the duck. Put mint jelly on the meat. (Also see Jellies, page 75.)

Tacos

Tacos are held in your hand and eaten very much as you would eat a hamburger.

Toast, English Muffins and Breadsticks

- While your toast is hot, it is okay to butter the entire piece of bread. Then you should break, or cut, your toast into bite-size pieces.

- If you put jam or jelly on your toast, you should use your butter knife or regular knife to apply the jelly or jam. Apply your jelly or jam to no more than what would be one or two bites at a time.

- English muffins should be treated the same way, buttered while hot, then broken into small bite sizes.

- Breadsticks should be buttered, one bite at a time.

Tortillas and Lefse

- Tortillas and Lefse are both thin, soft, pancake-like breads. Tortillas are thought of as a Latin American food. Lefse is thought of as Scandinavian food.

- Tortillas and Lefse can be laid out flat on your plate and buttered. They may be rolled up, held in your hand, and eaten as a bread along with other foods.

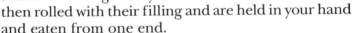

- Also, Tortillas and Lefse may be laid out flat on your plate and filled with any available filling. They are then rolled with their filling and are held in your hand and eaten from one end.

School

I n school you learn better when you have self respect and respect for others. School is the workplace of young people and, like any workplace, has rules and regulations to follow. Even so, fifteen minutes in any classroom will reveal which children have brought their good manners with them and which children have left them at home—or never learned them. In school, you can get a bonus for good manners: better grades. In the following list, which items are likely to affect your grades?

In the Classroom and Halls

- Listen to your teachers; follow their instructions.
- Avoid drumming, pulling fingers, biting nails, pulling or playing with your hair (or anyone elses).
- Don't whisper or chat while the teacher is talking or during study periods or tests.
- Don't kick open a door. Open a door with your hand. There are times when a door can be gently pushed open with a shoulder or elbow if your hands are full. *Never kick open* a door. To do so is crude, rude and thoughtless over and above the damage to the door.
- Close the door gently; don't slam it.
- Avoid goofing off or making a spectacle of yourself, unless it's recess or a play period.

- Cover your nose and mouth for sneezes or coughing and say "Excuse me."
- Raise your hand and wait to be recognized before speaking.
- Don't interrupt others while they are speaking.
- Don't pick your nose or teeth or spit.
- Respect personal property and school property. Report anything you have broken by mistake.
- Don't be an "elephant" going up and down stairs. Don't run in hallways.
- When you and your friends are walking through the hallways, don't "hog" the hall.
- When someone has helped you, say "Thank you." When you need help or a favor, say "Please."

With Other Students

- Take your turn in a line that's formed. To "cut in" or "budge" in a line is cheating, even if you are joining a friend who is already in line.
- Never make fun of another student or join in when others do.
- Ask permission to borrow items and return them on time and in good repair. Replace anything that you have broken or ruined.
- In general, avoid borrowing or lending money. If you do borrow or lend money, write down the transaction and have both parties sign a note. This is a contract. It helps to make clear what each one is saying and helps to avoid arguments.
- Don't use inappropriate or "foul" language around others. It reflects on you and only makes you look crude and ignorant.

- Avoid starting or passing rumors, especially if they ridicule another student. One day you could be the one being talked about.

- Hats and caps are for outside wear. Always remove them indoors.

- Be a friend and you'll always have friends. That means to follow the golden rule and treat others as you would like to be treated.

At Lunchtime

- Don't trade food, especially food that has been opened or nibbled on. That's unsanitary.

- Take small bites and chew with your mouth closed.

- Use a napkin, not your clothes, to wipe fingers and mouth.

- Talk quietly and take turns with others. Be a good listener. Don't interrupt.

- Ignore rude or loud talk and behavior. Laughing or responding will encourage attention-seekers to do even more.

- If you don't like a food, simply don't eat it. Don't throw it or drop it on the floor. Avoid "playing" with it. If you carry a sack lunch, ask your parent or caregiver to give you a substitute next time.

- If your school has a recycling program, show respect to the earth by recycling your garbage and paper.

Parties

Giving a Party—Going to a Party

Most of the parties that you will be giving or going to now will be birthday parties. When you are older, you will be giving and going to a variety of parties including dances and receptions. The guidelines and rules about good manners that you are learning and using now are a solid base for your good manners when your are older. It is important that you learn and practice now so that you will be comfortable going to or giving any kind of party.

Hosts, hostesses and guests who use good manners and know how to act at parties have more fun. You will have more fun at your own party if you know what to do and your host, hostess and other guests will enjoy you much more when you are a pleasant and enjoyable guest.

Planning a Party

- The first thing you do to plan a party is to talk with your parents or caregiver about the date. Then decide what kind of party and where you shall have the party. The next step is to decide how many friends you can invite.

- Even though it's pleasant and fun to be invited to a party, it's unkind and hurtful to talk about any party or plans in front of another friend who might not have been invited. It's a good idea not to talk with other friends about a party to which you are invited. Afterward, you will know who was there. After the party, it's still unkind to talk about a party in front of someone who was not included.

- If you hear about a party to which you are not invited, you must not ask for an invitation. Perhaps your friend can have only a limited number of guests this time, because of space in the house or costs, or perhaps the adult in charge is controlling your friend's guest list for reasons about which you haven't a clue. Just try not to feel too left out.

- You'll need to discuss the party and whether you can go or not, with your mother, father, or caregiver. The person responsible for you needs to help you arrange your transportation, the clothes you will wear and, if it's a birthday party, the gift that you will take.

- What to wear will depend on your age, the time of the year and the activities that are planned. Some parties are dress-up parties and some are active sports parties. Always be neat, clean and have on fresh clothing, no matter what activity is planned.

Invitations

- Make a guest list. You can include people who know each other well, but it's also fun to include a newcomer if it's someone you like and think your friends might also like. (Remember, we all may be or have been newcomers at some time or another.)

- Invitations should go out at least one week ahead of time. With your busy schedules and parents' busy schedules, ten days or two weeks is not too far ahead, particularly for written invitations. Written invitations are best simply because they have less chance for mistakes in time, address, place and telephone number. Remember to always mention what kind of a party it is so your guests will know what to expect and what to wear.

- Invitations can be received by mail, by telephone, or by direct conversation. If the invitation is written, it will have your host or hostess' telephone number and address on it. You may telephone or write a note with your response, but you need to make sure they receive your answer.

- When you receive an invitation to a party, or any special event, you might see the letters R.S.V.P. on the invitation. These letters mean: *Respondez s'il vous plait.* Respond if you please. The favor of a reply is requested. All R.S.V.P. invitations require an answer within two days after you receive the invitation.

- All invitations require a prompt answer unless the invitation states otherwise. The answer can be written or telephoned.

- If you've invited a friend to a party at your house and they call to say they can't come, don't just hang up; have a short conversation with them. You might say, "I'm sorry that you can't come. We will miss you and I'll see you later." That way your friend doesn't feel so left out. They are feeling badly enough to miss your party. They don't need you to be rude on the phone too!

Hosting a party

- Answering the door: The host or hostess opens the door wide and invites the guest in. "Hello, Meagen, please come in!" If it's a birthday party and you are the guest, you should say "Happy Birthday" as you come in through the door. Give your friend your gift as you enter. (Be sure you have a card taped or, somehow secured so your friend knows from whom the gift is given when opening their presents. It also helps with the writing of thank-you notes.)

- When you are host or hostess, be sure to say "Thank you" when you are given a gift. If you are given a gift at the door, put it with the others to be opened later.

- You are never too young to shake hands with your guests. By the time you are six or eight, you and your friends will be remembering to shake hands as you greet your guests at the door. Also, shake hands with your guests when they leave at the end of a party.

- If you are host or hostess, you and the adult in charge should be near the door with you until all the guests are greeted.

Introductions at a Party

- Introduce each guest to your parent or adult in charge. Also, introduce any other grown-ups who do not know each other. Introduce your guests to other adults who might be there.

- You should be sure that all friends are introduced. "Sam Howard, this is Enrique Ortiz—Enrique Ortiz, this is Sam Howard." "Mary Burns, this is Sam." (Remember, the girl's name comes first. If you can't remember a friend's last name don't worry. Just use a first name.

- If your guests are wearing coats, tell them where they might put them after the introductions, or you can take the coats from guests and hang them or put them in a bedroom.

Party Games

Party games should be fun. When playing party games, be a good sport. Join in the games and be pleasant even if you don't like the game.

If you are the host or hostess and win the game prize, don't keep the prize. Automatically, gracefully and quickly give it to the second-place winner. Everyone will like you better—including you.

Seating—Place Cards

"Place cards" are little cards with guests' names on them. Place cards are put at each place to show where each guest should sit at the table. Don't change the cards around; just sit where the card shows you to sit.

Eating at the Party

When you are host or hostess, the food is passed to your guests first. Never make a remark about any of your guests' manners or eating habits. Remember, everyone else is also learning good manners. You don't want to hurt anyone's feelings or embarrass anyone.

• Even though you have a good time at parties, you must remember good table manners. It's best that you wait for everyone to be seated and the host or hostess to start eating before you do.

• If you are not seated at a table for refreshments, and need to serve yourself, handle your plate and food carefully. If you should spill or drop anything, try to pick it up as best you can. Don't make a big fuss about it and embarrass everyone. If you become embarrassed, don't try to make a big joke out of it or do something silly or foolish to try to cover it up. Just confess to your host, hostess or adult in charge that you have a problem.

- When you are a guest and you have to leave the table, for any reason, you don't have to explain. Just say "excuse me"—put your napkin in your chair, leave quietly and return to the table without fanfare.

Goodbyes

- The time to leave a party is generally written on the invitation. Even though it might be fun, never linger after others have gone. As you leave a party, be sure and thank your friend and their parents or adult in charge. Example: "Thank you, Mrs. Chen. Thank you, Kitty, I really had a nice time."

- When you are the host or hostess, be sure to stand close to the door so your guests can say goodbye. Your "goodbyes" are as important as your "hellos."

- Remember to thank your guest for the present and shake hands as you say goodbye.

Dancing at Parties

- You probably won't be going to dances until you are around eleven or twelve years old, which is middle-school age.

- It is possible that you will be starting to attend a dancing school class about the time you are ten. These lessons teach you good manners, basic dance steps, basic rhythm and body coordination. Also, you'll learn the basic good manners of attending a dance or a formal ball. These are good things to know for the rest of your life.

- If dancing classes are not readily available, get your older brother, sister, cousins, mother, father or a grandparent to teach you the basic steps. How to dance is an agreeable nicety that we all should be able to do with ease and confidence. You can enjoy dancing at any age and most any place in the world.

Thank-You Notes

Thank-you notes need to be written for:

- *any gift received*
- *any party you've attended*
- *any overnight, weekend or vacation visit*
- *any flowers you've received*
- *any especially thoughtful thing that someone has done for you.*

The note doesn't need to be a long letter. It is nice if you can mention something about the gift or the visit in the note. See the examples on the following pages.

As you get older, you will probably have some personal stationery. Your thank-you notes can be written on personal stationery, a correspondence card of some kind, or whatever you might choose. Try not to use the notes that have "Thank you" already printed on them and a saying inside. These notes are not in the best of taste. However, if that is all you have, it is much better than no note at all. Just add your own written note for a more personal touch. Plain cards and papers or stationery with your name printed, embossed or engraved on them is the best to use for thank-you notes.

Thank-you notes are always written by hand (not on the word processor, etc.), even if your handwriting is difficult to read. They don't need to be long letters.

may 19, 1995
Dear Aunt Lucy,
Thank you for
the neat roller
skates that you sent
to me for my
birthday. I've had a
few falls, but
I'm learning fast.
Love,
Elaine

Dear Mrs. Speer,
Thankyou for the nice
weekend! I enjoyed being
there. The best part of
all was the great airplane
ride!

Yours Truly
Shannon

5/30/97

Dear Grandma,
How did you know I
was wishing for Legos?
Thank you very much.
Love,
Jaime

Dear Uncle John,
The money was
great. Thank you.
Love,
Jessica

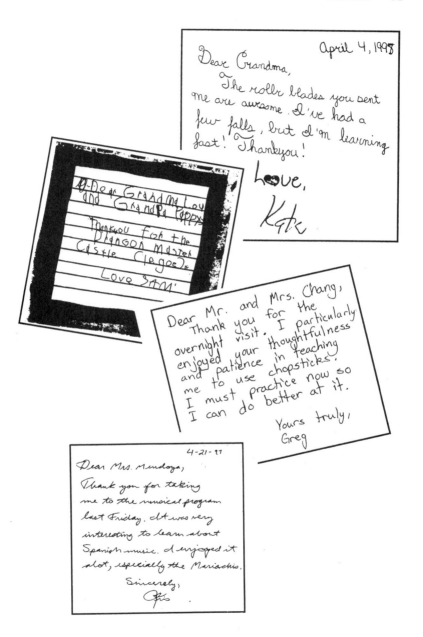

April 4, 1998

Dear Grandma,
The roller blades you sent me are awsome. I've had a few falls, but I'm learning fast! Thankyou!

Love,
Kate

Dear Grandma Lou
and Grandpa Pappy

Thankyou for the
Dragon Master
Castle (legoes)

Love Sam

Dear Mr. and Mrs. Chang,
Thank you for the overnight visit. I particularly enjoyed your thoughtfulness and patience in teaching me to use chopsticks! I must practice now so I can do better at it.

Yours truly,
Greg

4-21-97

Dear Mrs. Mendoza,
Thank you for taking me to the musical program last Friday. It was very interesting to learn about Spanish music. I enjoyed it alot, especially the Mariachis.

Sincerely,
Chris

Out and About

Arrival at the Restaurant

- Use the "coat check" if your coat is a heavy one for cold weather. A "coat check" is the place where you leave your coat and you receive a claim ticket so you can reclaim your coat when you leave. Sometimes there is either a small charge or an expected "tip" for the coat-check person.

- Wait at the entrance of the dining area for the head-waiter or the hostess to assign your group to a table. The women and girls follow the headwaiter and the men and boys come behind.

- If there is no headwaiter, an adult, generally the host or hostess, finds a suitable table.

- Sit where it is suggested that you sit. Don't make a fuss about sitting next to someone. If, for some reason, it is important that you sit next to someone, quietly mention it to your mother, father or the adult in charge before you reach the table.

- Women and girls are seated first. Their chairs are pulled out either by the headwaiter, by the host, or by the father. The mother or older woman is seated first. Then the younger women and girls are seated, being assisted by host, the younger men and boys or maître d'hôtel. If there are more women and girls than men, then the older women are seated first. The girls and women either wait their turn, or generally, start to seat themselves. After the women and girls are seated, the men and boys seat themselves. The seating is done the same in a restaurant as it is at home. Be cooperative and help avoid confusion.

- A gentleman always removes his hat or cap in a restaurant. If there is a coat check, he leaves it there.

- In a casual restaurant there may be no coat check. If you find no safe place to put or hang a raincoat or topcoat and hat, you must take them to the table and put them on the back of the chair. A hat can be placed under the chair.

- A gentleman never removes his suit jacket or blazer jacket while he is at the table.

- A boy or man always unbuttons his suit jacket or blazer jacket when he sits. When he stands, he buttons one button of the suit jacket, blazer jacket or sport coat. The same procedure is used for a double-breasted jacket.

- Purses: Purses, gloves, and handkerchiefs should never be put on the table. Put them in your lap, behind you in the chair or under the front part of your chair behind your feet throughout the meal. Be careful that they or their handles and straps are not in the walking and stepping area of the waiter.

Napkins

In a restaurant, your napkin is handled the same way it is at home. The host or hostess picks his or hers up as soon as seated and places it in the lap, then you place yours in your lap. (See Napkins, page 54.)

Menus

- Each person will receive a menu. In a formal restaurant, generally, the host or hostess should order for everyone. Sometimes when you are older and a boy and girl are alone in a formal restaurant, the boy asks the girl what she wants and then gives the waiter both orders. In a less formal restaurant, it is expected and acceptable for the girl to go ahead and order when the waiter turns to her.

- If you are part of a large group, in a casual restaurant, order when it's your turn. It is also proper to ask an adult to help you if you are younger.

General Guidelines

- Only the host or hostess should call for the waiter's attention. When you are out to dinner with adults, let them speak to the waiter for you.

- If you have an accident at the table, the host, hostess, or you, if you are older, quietly gets the waiter's attention. Let the waiter take care of it and don't make a big issue of it. Just say, "I'm sorry."

- It is not necessary to thank the waiter or waitress every time they bring a different dish. If they ask you if you want something, say "No, thank you" or "Yes, please."

- If you drop silverware or something from the table on the floor, ask your host, or the adult with you, to ask the waiter for another one. *Leave* the article that you dropped on the floor. Do not pick up anything from the floor. The waiter will pick it up unobtrusively before or after you leave.

- If someone stops by the table to talk, men and boys always rise, shake hands, and remain standing while the other person is present.

- If someone stops to talk at your table, everyone at the table is introduced.

- Girls remain seated, except when an older woman stops to talk. Then the young girl stands also. (A good gauge of age is, if the woman is about your mother's age or older, then, if you are a girl, you should stand.)

- An adult with good manners will make their "stops" and "hellos" *very* brief so people at the table won't feel an obligation to stand.

- If you ask the waiter for something, remember the word "please."

- Water glasses are not finger bowls. Napkins or fingers should never be dipped in them.

- When you are finished, you may not excuse yourself from the table the way you do at home. Sit at the table until it's time to go. If you join the conversation, or are a good listener, it is a more enjoyable time for you and for the others at the table.

- When it's time to go, leave your napkin on the table on the left-hand side. Don't refold it. Just put it on the table casually, the same way you do at home.

- If you are younger than ten or eleven and need to be excused to go to the bathroom, you may not go alone. An adult should go with you. Quietly indicate your need to the appropriate adult.

- The tip is always left by the "host" person. (The host person is the one who is paying the bill.)

- Never discuss the bill or the tip. The host or hostess will take care of it.

- If there are coats to be put on, the men and boys always help the women and girls with them in the foyer or waiting area, not at the table area.

- The men and boys always precede the women and

girls out of the restaurant and hold the door open for them.

- The men and boys open the car doors for the women and girls and get in after they do.

- The driver should double-check to determine that all seat belts are fastened.

- Always remember a sincere "Thank you" to your host or hostess for the nice dinner and lovely evening out. Adults need to know they are appreciated, too.

- If you are seated at a lunch counter or movie theater, offer to move over a seat when the place where you are sitting would separate two people who wish to sit together.

Holding the Door

If you are a boy, it's okay to hold the door open for a girl and let her go through first. There was a time a few years ago when some women didn't want the door held for them, but good manners are always in style.

If you're a girl, it's okay to let the boy open the door for you, but if you see that the boy's hands are full then open the door for him.

Whether you are a boy or a girl, opening the house door or a car door for an older person is the polite thing to do. Let thoughtfulness and common sense guide you in each situation.

Elevators

- If you are waiting for an elevator and you see people who want to get off the elevator when the doors open, wait until they get off before you get on.

- If you are in the elevator and someone in the back wants out, either step to one side or step out of the elevator until they get off and then step back on.

- If an elderly person or a disabled person needs help, ask if you may help them. This is the thoughtful and courteous thing to do.

- An elevator is considered an inside room. Therefore, if you are a man or boy, you remove your hat or cap while you are in the elevator. If the elevator is extremely crowded it is permissible to leave it on. People will understand why you have not removed it.

Escalators

- Even though it's tempting, *don't* play on an escalator. It's rude, thoughtless and dangerous.

- Don't walk or run up or down an escalator *against* its moving direction.

- It is acceptable to walk up or down an escalator when you go in the *same* direction that the escalator is going.

- When others are on the escalator, be patient. Don't try to crowd past them. If you wish to pass say "Excuse me." Pass on the left side. If you are standing, stand to the right so others may pass on your left.

Moving Walkways

- *Never* run on a moving walkway.

- If you wish to pass someone who isn't walking, or who is walking more slowly than you are walking, pass them on their left side, saying "Excuse me." If they are blocking your way, just say "Excuse me, on the left."

- If you wish to stand still on the moving walkway, stand on the right side of the walkway so others can pass you on your left side.
- Walk in the same direction the moving walkway is going. *Don't* walk on it in the opposite direction.
- If you are with a group, stand or walk in a single file. Don't stand two or three abreast.

Other People's Rights

- When in public play your cassette player, radio, Walkman, or personal stereo with head phones. Play it softly so that no one around you is annoyed or bothered. Remember that not everyone may enjoy the same music you do.
- When you are in a crowd be considerate. Move carefully. Try not to bump into, push or shove people. Be especially considerate of people with wheelchairs, baby strollers, canes or anything else that makes crowds difficult for them.
- When you are walking on the street, boys and men walk on the curb side of the sidewalk. If there are two girls and a boy, the boy still walks on the curb side. It is a nicety that is a custom that stems from a man's protective measures in past history, and it is still a polite thing to do.
- Bikes, skateboard, roller skates and roller blades are fun. The problems come when you forget that the people walking on the sidewalk have the first right to be there. Some places have restrictions on where you can ride or skate. Follow the rules and always remember to respect other people's rights.

Eating from a Buffet

A *buffet* (pronounced bu-fay)—is a counter or table where food and drinks are served.

- You serve yourself from the buffet and then carry your plates to another place to sit and eat. Sometimes a buffet is used when there is a crowd in a home. Many restaurants use this method of service.

- When you are quite small and not able to carry your plate or handle the service spoons, an adult will probably help you. As you become older, you can help yourself.

- Women and girls always go first in the line.

- Take a plate and walk by the buffet table taking small to medium helpings of the food that you think you will like. You can always go back for seconds.

- You generally make at least three trips to the food table. The first trip will be for the salad or soup course. On your second trip to the service table for your hot entrée (main course), there will probably be a chef waiting there to help you with hot food and/or (particularly) the meat. Let them help you! Your third trip to the table will probably be for dessert. Your milk or other drinks are generally ordered from and brought to the table, by the waiter. Even though you might be the first to arrive at the table with your food, it is a nice and polite gesture to wait until others have also come to the table before you begin eating your food. If your host or hostess tells you to go ahead and start eating and not to wait for everyone, then do so.

- Each time you go to the buffet food table, leave your used dishes on the table where you've eaten. The waiter will clear them before you return to the table.

- Put your napkin in your chair between courses. Your napkin goes on the table only when the meal is finished and you are leaving the table to leave the restaurant.

Afternoon Tea

When I was young my mother used to say to me, "Learn good manners and practice how to not make sounds when you drink or sip your tea, because someday you may be invited to have tea with the Queen." You may not receive an invitation for tea with the Queen but afternoon tea is once again gaining in popularity. In an elegant hotel tea can be quite formal or in a home more casual. No matter where the setting you should be clean, neatly dressed and use your best manners. It is served between 3:30 and 5:00 p.m. Do not mistake the term "High-tea" for afternoon tea. "High-tea" is an English term that refers to a working man's "cold supper" generally of leftovers from the noon meal. Afternoon tea consists of tea served with milk (not cream), sugar or lemon. Hot chocolate is sometimes served if younger people who don't drink tea are to be included.

Finger sandwiches, scones, some kind of cake or fruit tartlets and a candy sweet are served. One may be tempted to devour the small tea sandwiches in one bite—but don't! The scones are eaten after the sandwiches. They are cut in half and then spread, one bite at a time, with butter, jam and cream, which is served in dishes for the whole table. Place a small amount of each on your side plate using the serving utensils that are in the serving dishes. You will be provided with a small knife. Use it to spread the butter, jam and cream. If you are served cake, a fork will be provided.

The "Star Spangled Banner" and Flag

We pledge allegiance to the United States flag because it is the symbol of our country. When we pledge allegiance to the flag or our national anthem, the "Star

Spangled Banner," is played, everyone should stand at attention (and most properly of all, with the right hand over the heart). Standing at attention means no talking, whispering or giggling. Boys and men should remove their hat, cap or any other head covering. This is done to show respect.

Attending Churches, Synagogues and Other Holy Places

Places of worship, whatever the religion, are usually orderly, quiet and calm. You show your respect to your church, or, if visiting, to your friend's church, by having good manners when you attend a service.

- Dress in clothes that are neat, clean and uncluttered. Example: Lots of bracelets that jangle when you move, or a scarf, or something that gets caught when you kneel or sit, can be distracting and annoying to those near you. Consider not wearing perfume or cologne. If you do wear a scent, go easy on the amount.

- Be a few minutes early, if possible, so you can select the seats you prefer. There is generally someone there to help you find a seat. If there is no usher when you go down the aisle, the man of the family goes first, selects the seats and then stands aside so the family can be seated. If there is an usher, the women go first behind the usher. If there is no usher and no one to help, just quietly find a seat.

- You should stop talking when you enter a holy place. Save questions, comments and conversation until after the service.

- Even if you don't fully understand the service, sit quietly and listen. When you giggle, fidget, whisper, play a quiet game, or fiddle with gadgets, you are annoying the people around you. (If a little person is under two or three, they are generally taken to a nursery.)

- In a strange church, don't criticize or question what is happening *while* it is happening. If you are confused about sitting, standing, kneeling, or other rituals, wait and do as the others do. It is also acceptable to just sit quietly and not join in the rituals. Afterward, find out about the customs and rituals. There are many varied religions in this world and it's interesting and educational to learn about many of them. There will generally be adults around who can explain the rituals and the customs.

Bar-Mitzvah and Bat-Mitzvah

A "bar-mitzvah" for a boy and a "bat-mitzvah" for a girl are solemn Jewish religious ceremonies celebrated at the age of thirteen for boys and at the age of twelve or thirteen for girls. It is an important celebration with family and friends; therefore it is usually followed immediately with a festive reception.

For this solemn service in the synagogue and celebration afterward, you should be well dressed. Boys should wear a suit and tie. Young male guests are generally provided skullcaps to be worn during the service. Girls should be dressed in an appropriate dress. Pants are not in the best of taste in the synagogue. Girls do not wear headcoverings..

Any gift suitable for a boy or girl's birthday is appropriate for a bar-mitzvah or bat-mitzvah gift. It's best to send or take your gift to your friend's home the day before or the day after the celebration. It is not appropriate to take your gift to the synagogue or to give your gift the day of the celebration.

A boy becomes a "bar-mitzvah" or a girl a "bat-mitzvah." The parents celebrate his "bar-mitzvah" or her "bat-mitzvah."

At the reception or party for your friend remember to congratulate your friend on his "bar-mitzvah" or her "bat-mitzvah." Introduce yourself and shake hands. Introduce those who might not know each other at the party. Use your best manners.

Weddings

A wedding is one of the most important events of an adult's life. When you attend a wedding you should be neat, clean and well-dressed.

Arrive a few minutes early. You will be shown to your seat by an usher. If there is no usher quietly choose a seat. If you are to be a part of the ceremony, clothes will be chosen for you and you will be instructed as to what is expected of you. Honor your invitation by using your best manners during the services and the party afterward.

Funerals: Death in the Family

The time of a funeral is a sad and lonesome time for adults as well as children. Notes, flowers, funeral attendance and home calls let you know that you are not alone in your time of sadness.

Even though death is a natural part of life, it is hard to know what to say or what to do when there is a death of a family member, a friend, or in the family of someone you know. People of all ages often do not know how to handle their feelings and grief.

Many times we experience some consolation and comfort from the words of praise or words of remembrance from friends about our loved ones. There is emotional support knowing that others share our grief.

- Don't worry about what you are supposed to do. Wherever the funeral is to be conducted, you will be told what to do, such as where to sit.

- Be quiet and respectful.

- Remember to carry a handkerchief or tissues.

- Don't be ashamed of or embarrassed by tears or quiet crying. It's a normal reaction to grief by a person of any age.

- Children under the age of twelve or thirteen are not expected to make condolence calls to another family. (Condolence means sympathy.) However, if children six or seven years old, or older, have a close friend whose mother, father, grandparent, brother or sister has died, it would be reassuring to have a playmate come to call (and stay a few minutes) and say, "I'm sorry about your brother—sister—grandmother." A written note saying the same thing would help the one who is grieving.

- If you are the one who is receiving the condolence just say "Thank you," and invite your friend in for a few minutes. You and your friend may be at a loss for words at first, but just talk about normal everyday things. Example: "What did you do at school today?"

- Any time we want to show our respect, we are neat,

clean, use our best manners and wear our best clothes. We do the same thing to dress for a funeral.

- By the entrance door or in the hall at the entrance of the place of the funeral, there is generally a book or list in which you sign your name. Please do this because it is a keepsake to help the family remember who attended the funeral.

- Sometimes, either before or after the funeral, there is a receiving line. When you go through the line, shake hands, give the people in line your name and some short sympathy comment to the immediate family members. Example: "I'm Tyler Johnson, I knew Molly in school. We will all miss her."

- If you can't think of anything to say, it is acceptable to just go through the line, shake hands and say, "I'm Tyler Johnson." A pat on the shoulder or a hug are sometimes as good as words. They convey your feelings. The very fact that you are there lets your friend know that you do care and respect his or her feelings.

If a Pet Dies

If you have a pet that dies, you also are sad and need to grieve.

- If your friend's pet dies, you need to tell your friend that you are sorry about his or her pet. Maybe even recount a funny story about the pet, such as, "Remember how Bonzo rolled in the mud puddle and then shook the muddy water all over us?"

- In any death, you help your friend's grieving process by recognizing his or her sorrow.

Theater, Concert
and Ballet

Someone once said that the difference between the movies and the theater is that "movies" are pictures and "theater" is live people on the stage performing for us. This is true.

- Dress in your good clothes. Be clean and neat. A dress for girls and a blue blazer, shirt and tie and grey trousers are appropriate for boys. If you don't have a blue blazer, then a nice jacket or a nice sweater and tie are acceptable most of the time.

- Arrive in time to be seated before the program begins. It's an insult to the performers to arrive late.

- In the cold weather when you wear heavy coats, it is a good idea for you to "check" your coat at the coat check, if possible, rather than to wrestle with your coat while you are in your seat. Most theaters and concert halls have coat-check facilities available.

- Ushers will usually lead you to your seat after you give them your tickets. (Generally, you will be with an adult and the adult hands the usher all of the tickets.)

- If you are given the ticket stub, be sure to keep it. You will need it to return to your seat if you should, for some reason, have to go out at intermission.

- When an usher leads you to your seat, the women and girls follow immediately behind the usher, then the men and boys.

- If you arrive late and the performance has started, the usher will ask you to wait until there is a pause in the program before he or she will seat you. Do not expect them to do otherwise.

- If there is no usher, the host, man, or older boy takes the place of the usher as you walk down the aisle. He finds the row, then steps aside so the women can go in first. A man or boy always sits next to the aisle.

- If you have to cross in front of someone, say "Excuse me, please." Try not to step on toes.

- If someone goes across in front of you when you are seated, if you are a boy, stand and if you are a girl turn your knees to the side.

- Intermission is a 10- to 15-minute break in the program. You may go to the restroom, get a drink or just stay at your seat. It's perfectly proper, and generally good, to stand up and move a little right at your seat.

- Applause is your way of "thanking" the performers. Clapping is the preferred applause. (Sometimes people whistle and stomp their feet, but that is generally thought of as uncouth and rude). At a play, you applaud at the end of each act. At a concert or ballet, you applaud at special times; including when the conductor walks on stage and bows to the audience, and when each musical selection is completed.

- Most musicals and concerts have several parts with pauses in between. It is wise to watch the conductor. He will turn and face the audience when each selection is finished. Applaud at that time.

- Boys and girls applaud (clap) differently. A girl applauds by forming a shallow cup with her left hand and sort of "spanks" it with her right hand. A boy applauds with the palms of his hands flat. (These are definitely kind of "old-fashioned" gentlemanly and lady-like tips, but I think they are nice to know.)
- Remember to thank whoever took you. Going to the theater, concert or ballet is thought of as an extra special treat, whether or not you happened to like the performance.

Movies

- At the movie, always be considerate of those around you, even if you don't like the movie. Others might be enjoying the movie. Don't spoil it for them.
- Gum smacking and blowing bubbles is totally unacceptable.
- If others are already seated and you need to pass in front of them, say "Excuse me" and don't step on their feet as you go by.
- Popcorn, candy bars and soft drinks have become standard snacks at the movies. Eat and drink them quietly. Put empty containers in garbage cans as you leave.
- Talking, giggling or loud whispers are annoying to others.
- Never put your feet on or kick the back of the seat in front of you.
- Wait until the movie is entirely over before you get your things together to go or put on coats.
- If you were someone's guest at the movie, remember to say "Thank you."

Sports and Games

Many sports and games are considered a "party" or social function, not a sport and are nice activities to know how to do. Knowing how to play many different sports and games can open many social doors for you when you are young and can continue to open doors for you for the rest of your life. When you learn to play sports and games, it makes it easier and more pleasant for others to include you in group activities.

Learning and following all of the rules of the game is an important part of your instructions when you take lessons or when you learn by playing with your friends or parents.

Many sports require special equipment, lessons and a special place or environment in which to learn. When learning sports, pay attention to the person instructing you and follow the rules. There are few things that are more irritating to an instructor than a "goof off." Being a "goof off" can also be irritating to the people with whom you are playing and your classmates. If you learn to participate with integrity, fairness, and character, then you will receive the kind of attention that gladdens your heart and makes your friends and family proud of you no matter how well you play.

Everyone enjoys playing with a good sport. You are a good sport if you play to the best of your ability, but when you lose you are gracious and pleasant. Don't blame others for your losses. Compliment your opponents when they win.

When you win don't be a braggart or "smart-alec," no matter how elated you may feel. When you finish always say "Thank you, I enjoyed playing with you." It is a nice gesture to shake hands with those with whom you have played.

Visiting Overnight

You should feel complimented when you are asked to visit a friend's house for overnight or for a weekend.

- You should accept the invitation only after a parent or person in charge from both families have talked together about the arrangements.
- You should know at what time you should arrive and at what time you should depart.
- You should also know who will take you, who will bring you home, and what activities are planned, if any. That way there will be no misunderstandings about your arrival, your departure, or the clothes to pack.

Packing

You should pack in one suitcase all the personal things that you might need: toothbrush, toothpaste, comb and hairbrush, night clothes, robe, slippers and clothes. Check with your host or hostess to see if you need a sleeping bag and pillow. Try not to borrow personal items unless you find it definitely necessary.

House Gift

- If you are a house guest for longer than overnight,

it's nice to take a "house gift," something for the parents, or something for the family to share.

- If you didn't take a house gift with you, then an appropriate gift can be sent by you, with the help of your mother, father or person in charge. This should be sent soon after you've returned home.
- Sometimes flowers with a note from you is a thoughtful way of saying "Thank you."
- Remember that a thank-you note is required.

Unpacking at Your Friends

- When you arrive unpack your suitcase and put your things where you are shown.
- During your visit keep your personal belongings in the space allotted to you. This way it's easier to keep track of your things while you are visiting, and it's easier to pack, and go home without leaving something behind. It's a terrible nuisance for your host or hostess to have to return things to you if you leave something behind.

Telephone

Never—use the phone without asking permission. If you do have to use the phone, make your call brief.

Food

When you are served new foods, you should take a small amount and at least taste them.

Rules

- In a friend's home, you always follow the "House Rules" made by their parents or adult in charge. It isn't proper to say "We never eat that" or "We always go to bed later" or "My mother always lets me watch that TV program." Remember, you are a guest.

- Curiosity is human nature, and curiosity is one way in which we learn. However, when you are a guest in someone's home, *never* investigate someone else's cupboards, drawers, closets or letters. Private possessions are always "off limits" for you. Just think about how embarrassed you would be if you were caught looking in someone's drawers. How would you feel if you found your friend going through your mother's, sister's, or brother's personal things? It would be embarrassing for everyone.

Bathroom

When you leave the bathroom be sure you leave it neat. Also, don't stay in the bathroom an unnecessarily long time.

Bed

Make your own bed in the morning, even if there is a maid or housekeeper.

Homesickness

At some time in our lives, we all have had feelings of "homesickness." If this happens when you are visiting, just try to get busy with something, read or make an extra effort to join in the activities. Try not to concentrate on yourself and remember that this feeling will pass.

What If You Break Something?

If you accidentally break something, you shouldn't try to hide it. Tell one of your friend's parents or person in charge and apologize. The minute you get home, tell your parents and try to replace whatever it was that was broken. Accidents do happen to everyone at some-time or other.

Leaving

- Leave at the time of your planned departure even if you are having a wonderful time. Don't phone your parents or person in charge to ask if you can stay longer, even if your friend is urging you to do so. Say goodbye to every member of the family. If there is a cook, housekeeper and/or maid, remember to thank them also.

- Remember to write a thank-you note to your friend when you get home. It is an absolute "must do" to also write a thank-you note to your friend's parents when you get home, thanking them for the visit.

- Thank-you notes should be written promptly (within two days, if possible). If you are not old enough to write, you can still do something that says "Thank you." I know of one little boy who drew a picture with finger paints for his note. Of course, his mother wrote a note explaining the picture and signed his name. The hosts were pleased and touched. (Refer to thank-you notes, page 91.).

Conclusion

Even though people say nothing, they *do* notice the use of, or the lack of, good manners. Don't you? We all do.

Now that you have been introduced to basic good manners, *practice* them. Practice, practice, practice your manners so they become good habits.

Now that you know good manners, you are going to be surprised at how many people allow their manners to slip and do the inappropriate things. That's because they have not been taught basic good manners or have never bothered to learn and practice the simple rules of acceptable behavior and etiquette. *Never* point out other's bad manners. Just continue your own good manners.

At times, we all find ourselves in situations that we aren't sure how to handle. When this happens use good common sense. Don't be afraid to ask what is expected of you in a given situation.

Mistakes happen when it comes to manners, just like everything else. If you do make a mistake, just remember that "no one is perfect" and you can use the situation as a learning experience.

The "good manners golden rule" is—"Always treat others as you would like them to treat you." Be kind, courteous, thoughtful, pleasant and cheerful. When you are, you will like yourself and others will like you.

Bibliography

Applewood Books. *George Washington's Rules of Civility and Decent Behavior in Company and Conversation.* Bedford, MA: 1988.

Baldrige, Letitia. *The Amy Vanderbilt Complete Book of Etiquette, Revised and Expanded.* Garden City, NY: Doubleday and Company, 1978.

Baldrige, Letitia. *Complete Guide to Executive Manners.* NY: Rawsan Associates, and Collier Macmillan, Canada, Inc., 1985.

Baldrige, Letitia. *Complete Guide to the New Manners for the '90s.* New York: Rawson Associates, 1990.

Carter, Rosalynn and Markova, Dawna. *Kids Random Acts of Kindness.* Berkeley, CA: Conari Press, 1994.

de Pubillones, Lietty Raventos. *Sus Modales ¿de Ayer o de Hoy?* Costa Rica: Trejos Hermanos Sucesores, S.A., 1988

Hoving, Walter. *Tiffany's Table Manners for Teenagers.* New York: Random House, 1989.

Latner, Helen. *The Book of Modern Jewish Etiquette.* New York: Schocken Books, 1981.

Post, Elizabeth L. *Emily' Post's Advice for Every Dining Occasion.* New York: Harper Collins Publisher, Inc., 1994.

Post, Elizabeth L. *Emily Post's Etiquette (15th Edition).* New York: Harper-Collins, 1992.

Post, Emily. *Etiquette.* New York: Funk & Wagnalls Company, Publishers, Sixty-ninth Printing, 1947.

Shaw, Corolyn Hagner. *Modern Manners for All Occasions.* New York: E.P. Dutton & Company, Inc., 1958.

Vanderbilt, Amy. *Complete Book of Etiquette–A Guide to Gracious Living.* Garden City, NY: Doubleday & Company, Inc., 1954.